POMPEII

guide to the archaeological excavations

FLAVIVS

The Capitolium and in the foreground the remains of the colonnade of the Forum.

5   POMPEII AND ITS HISTORY

8   POMPEII, A TRAGIC DESTINY

10 THE BURIAL

13 THE FOLLOWING DAY

15 THE RETURN TO THE LIGHT

19 FROM PORTA MARINA TO THE TEMPLE OF
        FORTUNA AUGUSTA

43 FROM VIA DI MERCURIO TO
        PORTA ERCOLANO

59 FROM THE NECROPOLIS OF PORTA ERCO-
        LANO TO THE HOUSE OF THE VETTII

79 FROM THE HOUSE OF THE ANCIENT HUNT
        TO THE TEMPLE OF JUPITER MEILICHIOS

93 FROM THE TEMPLE OF ISIS TO
        PORTA STABIA

120 GLOSSARY
        TO FIND OUT MORE

The bronze statue of Apollo the archer.

POMPEII AND ITS HISTORY

> *"Pompeii stands at the mouth of the Sarno river, a port for the cities of Nola, Nuceria, and Acerrae, with a harbour suitable for trade."*
> **Strabo (63 BC – 24 AD)**

The foundation of the settlement that was to become Pompeii is dated between the end of the seventh and the early sixth century BC, and is attributed to the Oscans who populated the region. It is believed that the inhabitants of the various settlements located along the Sarno valley moved to the new city. The upland upon which it was founded, a plateau of hard volcanic lava set

Reconstruction of the Triangular Forum.

30 metres above sea level, made it particularly easy to defend, and its proximity to the Sarno river (which was navigable at the time) and its estuary rendered it an important seaport for the Greeks and the Phoenicians. Moreover, it was also situated at a strategic junction between the main cities of the area: Cumae, Nola, Nuceria and Stabiae. This felicitous combination of factors assured the city's rapid development and prosperity.

The most ancient religious buildings are the sanctuary dedicated to Apollo, and a temple dedicated to Athena and Hercules, both of Etruscan imprint, even though there are clear signs of the cultural influence that the Greek world exerted over both the Etruscans and the Italic races in general. The first wall circle and the initial regular layout of the settlement date to the first half of the sixth century BC. In this period the entire region was affected by the conflict between the Etruscans, who dominated the Campania hinterland, and the Greeks, who in the eighth century BC had founded the emporium of Pithekoussai on the island of Ischia, and later a polis at Cumae. The inevitable clash between the two powers ended with the defeat of the Etruscans at the battle of Cumae in 524 BC. Subsequently the Samnites – inhabitants of the mountainous areas of Irpinia and Samnium – began to expand towards the coast and throughout the Campania plain. In 423 BC they conquered Capua, and a few years later Cumae itself. Pompeii in its turn became subject to the influence of the new Samnite power, and at the end of the fifth century its institutions, language and customs were those of the Samnites.

Reproduction of the fresco showing a naval battle, from the portico of the Temple of Isis.

Vesuvius, with the archaeological area in the left foreground and the settlement of modern-day Pompeii on the right.

Between 343 and 290 BC the Samnites clashed with the nascent power of Rome in the course of three long and bloody military campaigns, finally submitting to utter defeat.

Pompeii thus came under the yoke of Rome, and when Hannibal invaded Italy (218-203 BC) seeking to rouse the Italic cities, Pompeii remained faithful to Rome. This loyalty enabled it to obtain the privileged condition of a *"socium"* of Rome, which allowed for a certain autonomy, the maintenance of the civic institutions and its own language. However, these privileges were then lost when Pompeii joined the ranks against Rome in the revolt of the Italic peoples of central Italy, and it was besieged and conquered by Publius Cornelius Sulla in 89 BC. After this it became a Roman colony with the name of *Colonia* Cornelia *Veneria Pompeianorum* (80 BC), adopting Latin as the official language, even though Oscan was not totally abandoned. As a colony, one of the situations Pompeii had to face was the arrival of numerous Roman war veterans, who settled partly in the city and partly in the surrounding countryside and succeeded in taking over control even of the civic institutions. This turning-point was marked by dramatic transformations in the layout and architecture of the city, such as the reconstruction of the Samnite Temple of Jupiter which was dedicated to the Capitoline triad (Jupiter, Juno and Minerva). The process of Romanisation was accompanied by economic growth which increased further when Augustus came to power in Rome in 27 BC.

In Pompeii the arrival of the Empire was illustrated by propagandist building, such as the construction of the building of the Eumachia and the Temple of Fortuna Augusta.

The economic benefits of the *pax augustea* generated further commercial development in Pompeii, with a consequent boost in wealth and wellbeing. The sumptuous decor of the House of the Vettii is an illustration of the fortunes of the mercantile bourgeoisie connected with Rome and the new Augustan policy.

General view of the excavations (G. De Simone - D. Capri).

POMPEII, A TRAGIC DESTINY

With excavations extending over 44 hectares, Pompeii is the only archaeological site that illustrates a city of the Roman period in its entirety.

Together with Stabiae, Herculaneum and Oplontis, Pompeii was destroyed by the eruption of Vesuvius on the morning of 24 August 79 AD (although recent discoveries suggest that the date of the eruption was 24 October).

Possibly the ancient peoples were unaware of the volcanic nature of the mountain that was famous for its luscious vineyards, and the eruption may have taken everyone by surprise. There had in fact been numerous warning signs of the catastrophe. In 62 AD a violent earthquake had caused grievous damage to the city, and other quakes of lesser intensity had continued up to 79 AD, but they had not been attributed to volcanic activity.

Pliny the Younger (61-114 AD) wrote to Tacitus apropos this: *"For several days past there had been earth tremors which were not particularly alarming since they are a frequent phenomenon in Campania...."*

When Pompeii was buried by Vesuvius, restoration works were in progress on numerous buildings to repair the damage caused by the earthquake.

The interior of the Museum of Pompeii prior to 1943.

The archaeological area and Vesuvius.

The date of 24th August is a truly unlucky day for ancient Pompeii. In 1943 a violent and unjustified Anglo-American bombardment caused extensive damage to numerous houses and monuments.
The Museum of Pompeii with its precious and irreplaceable finds was hit by a bomb and completely destroyed.

THE BURIAL

The bas-relief showing the Capitolium struck by the earthquake of 62 AD from the House of Caecilius Jucundus

Towards midday on 24 August 79 AD the mountain revealed its true nature and with a sinister rumble announced the end of life in the area of Vesuvius: gas and erupted pumice darkened the sky and fell to earth beginning to bury the city of Pompeii. The hail of volcanic material continued up to the following day and, along with the quakes that accompanied it, caused the roofs of the houses to collapse. In this scene of apocalyptic devastation, those who tried to escape immediately, setting off in the direction opposite to that of Vesuvius, had some chance of saving themselves. Instead, those who sought refuge in their homes or tarried to gather their valuables or sought escape routes less favoured by fate, were doomed to certain death. Towards dawn of the following day, the eruptive violence of the volcano began to abate, only to be followed by unexpected and lethal clouds of gas and burning ashes that began to pour down its sides, penetrating everywhere and annihilating any few survivors there may have been. Then all was silence.

The death of Pliny the Elder, circle of T. De Vivo, nineteenth century.

VESUVIUS

In the Middle Ages Vesuvius was considered to be "the mouth of hell"

Before the eruption of 79 BC, the profile of Vesuvius was in the form of a single cone cut off at the summit. Its present contour is the result of that terrible explosion and the others that followed it. The surrounding area has revealed traces of human presence since the third millennium BC, although the eruptive activity of the volcano interfered with the population of the district on numerous occasions.

The cone of Vesuvius seen from above.

Vesuvius is the most closely monitored active volcano on the planet, since paradoxically its slopes feature one of the highest residential densities in the world. The type of eruption that destroyed Pompeii is defined as "Plinian", named after the famous naturalist who died in 79 AD, and is characterised by a violent initial explosion. In this phase massive quantities of ashes, gas and lapilli erupt to form a column rising to a height of approximately 10-15 kilometres from the mouth of the volcano. Falling to the ground, this material covered Pompeii in a thick blanket about 4 metres deep.

When the volcanic pressure subsides, the collapse of the eruptive column generates pyroclastic flows, comprising the lethal surges (ashes and water vapour at extremely high temperature), that pour swiftly down the sides of the volcano with a devastatingly destructive impact, or the lahars (mudflows) that buried Herculaneum. Eruptions of the Plinian kind are documented prior to 79 AD, that closest in time dates to 3750 years ago and is known as the Pomici di Avellino eruption. Since 79 AD numerous eruptions of Vesuvius have been recorded, of both the effusive and the explosive type.

There was a particularly violent eruption in 1631, classified as a Subplinian eruption, when the lahars reached as far as the sea and permanently modified the coastline.

Volcanologists believe that the intervals between two Plinian eruptions can be particularly long because of the enormous quantity of energy and eruptive material that characterises them.

Panoramic view of Vesuvius and the Gulf of Naples from Mount Faito.

"Above these places lies Mount Vesuvius, which, save for its summit, has splendid country estates all around. As for the summit, a considerable part of it is flat, but all of it is infertile and looks like ashes, revealing porous cavities in masses of soot-coloured rock that look as though they had been burnt out by fire. Hence one might infer that in earlier times this district was on fire and had craters of fire, which then was quenched when the fuel gave out."
Strabo (63 BC-24 AD).

Reconstruction of Vesuvius before 79 AD. The dotted line shows the present profile.
Below: Karl Petrovich Brjullov. The Last Day of Pompeii, 1828/1834,
St. Petersburg.

THE FOLLOWING DAY

> *After the eruption, it no longer has any*
> *sense to speak of Pompeii: the city as such*
> *no longer exists....*
> **P.G. Guzzo**

When the fury of Vesuvius abated the daylight illuminated a scene of death: the landscape was covered with a grey mantle and all forms of life had disappeared. The enormous quantity of volcanic material had deviated the course of the Sarno river and shifted the entire coastline seaward.

Plaster cast of a door in the Villa of the Mysteries.

Several days after the eruption an imperial commission arrived in the Vesuvian area to assess the damage, and also set about retrieving what was possible: precious marbles, statues, sacred objects, travertine from the pavement of the Forum. Alongside these institutional attempts at recovery, private citizens too dug tunnels through the thick layer of lapilli and, making holes in the walls of the houses, attempted to retrieve precious objects, the bodies of their loved ones or any domestic furnishings that might still be useful. What is certain, however, is that the inhospitable desolation of the place soon drove them to take up their abode elsewhere.

In 80 AD the Emperor Titus visited the area and declared it vain to make any attempt to restore life to the cities that were by now irreparably buried.

In 106 AD Tacitus composed his "History", publishing the two letters that he had received from Pliny the Younger, an eye witness of the tragedy.

Around 120 AD the Emperor Hadrian rebuilt the road network in the area.

Excavations reveal the various layers of eruptive material that buried the city.

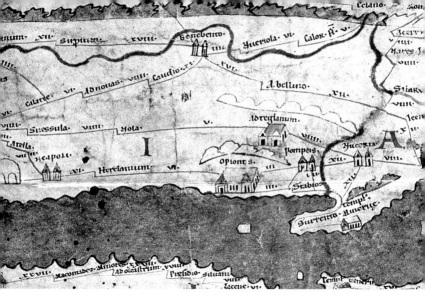

The Tabula Peutingeriana.

In one of his writings, the Emperor Marcus Aurelius cited the fate of Pompeii as an example of the frailty and precariousness of earthly life. At the beginning of the third century the historian Cassius Dio provided a new account of the disaster, which had returned to the general attention as a result of another violent eruption of Vesuvius. The Emperor Alexander Severus (208-235 AD) had the excavations resumed to retrieve marbles, columns and statues, but these works too were soon interrupted. A glancing reference to Pompeii persists in Roman cartography, and then nothing. It is probable that at the time of the eruption the city was not completely inhabited since many dwellings had been rendered uninhabitable by the earthquakes preceding the catastrophe that had ravaged the Vesuvian area for years before. The excavations have brought to light the remains of approximately two thousand human victims out of an estimated population of about 10,000 inhabitants.

...noramic view of the Forum, by G. Gigante.

THE RETURN TO
THE LIGHT

*The beginning of modern archaeology
is linked to the discoveries of
Herculaneum, Pompeii and Stabiae
between 1709 and 1749.*
P.G. Guzzo

*When in April 1748 the colonel Rocco Giocchino
de Alcubierre… obtained royal consent to
make exploratory excavations close to Torre
Annunziata, at the foot of the hill known as la
Civita, nobody imagined, being still ignorant of
the actual site of Pompeii, that this exploration
would have given rise to the greatest and
longest archaeological enterprise of the modern
age. The scanty and incomplete information
that circulated regarding the first discoveries in
fact referred either to the Campo della Civita or
to the Osteria del Lapillo or to the Pompeàna,
as if they were merely isolated villas or
buildings and not an authentic city…..*

A. Maiuri, Scoperta di Pompei, in *Le grandi
scoperte archeologiche*, Torino 1956

The thick blanket of ashes and lapilli sealed in the city, with its houses, its monuments and all the life stories of its inhabitants, thus preserving them for the curiosity of posterity.

The tragedy was documented by Pliny the Younger who watched the dramatic events from Cape Misenum, later immortalising them in two letters sent to Tacitus, the Roman historian who had asked him to recount the adventures of his uncle, Pliny the Elder, who had died in an attempt to save the people struck by the eruption.

A city suddenly buried two thousand years ago, a chronicler who describes the events and the excavations that restore them to us: these are the ingredients of the intriguing story that has enveloped ancient Pompeii from the time of its discovery.

In the sixteenth century, while excavating to construct a canal in the vicinity of the hill of Civita, the architect Domenico Fontana accidentally came across several buildings with decorated walls. In 1689, again in the area of Civita, walls and a number of epigraphs were found during the excavation of a well. It was in this area, where from time to time rumours circulated about accidental discoveries, that on the orders of Charles of Bourbon, the military engineer Roque de Alcubierre with the assistance of Karl Weber carried out the first excavation on 23 March 1748, bringing to light various finds and the first skeleton of one of the victims. Initially the explorations, which were erroneously believed to be on the site of the ancient Stabiae, did not follow a precise plan, and excavations were carried out sporadically at various points of the site. Interest frequently flagged, or shifted to Herculaneum where, despite the greater difficulties of excavating the extremely hard layer of solidified mud, sensational discoveries were coming to light, such as that in 1750 of the famous library of 1,800 papyri from the celebrated Villa dei Papiri. It was only in 1763, following the discovery of a cippus of Titus Suedius Clemens with a precise reference to the *Res Publica Pompeianorum* that the excavators realised that these were effectively the remains of ancient Pompeii. Charles of Bourbon, King of Naples at the time, grasped the importance of what was coming to light and set up in Portici the first museum to house the antiquities from Herculaneum and Pompeii, exerting himself for the continuation of the excavations. During this phase the finds that were considered of interest were taken away without documenting their discovery, while artefacts that were deemed to be of little interest or obscene were abandoned or even destroyed.

A collection of objects and paintings featuring erotic scenes and subjects was segregated in special rooms, with access reserved to nobility of the male sex provided with special authorisation from the sovereign. In the second half of the eighteenth century the area of the theatres, of the Triangular Forum and of the Temple of Isis was brought to light. In the north-western area of the city, the House of the Surgeon and the Villa of Diomedes were explored between 1760 and 1774; in the basements eighteen victims of the erup-

Excavation of a house in Pompeii, by L. Capaldo.

tion were discovered, along with a treasure of gold and silver coins. At the beginning of the nineteenth century the excavation works were resumed with renewed vigour under both Giuseppe Bonaparte and his successor Gioacchino Murat and his wife, Queen Carolina. During this phase the wall circle, the Basilica and the House of Pansa were discovered. After the Congress of Vienna and the return of Ferdinand of Bourbon to the throne of Naples, there was a loss of interest in Pompeii, although it was revived again under his son Francis I. Between 1820 and 1830 remarkable progress was made, and a series of sumptuous dwellings was brought to light, including the House of the Faun with the magnificent mosaic portraying Alexander the Great. In the meantime news of the sensational discoveries travelled round the world, with an enthralling and evocative impact, further fuelled by the circulation of the works of artists, intellectuals, draughtsmen and architects who came to Pompeii from all corners of the globe. Their works contributed to make the tragedy and the marvels of the buried city known, restoring to Pompeii a growing fascination in the collective imagination.

With the unification of Italy (1861) the direction of the excavation works was entrusted to Giuseppe Fiorelli who laid the foundations of scientific archaeology, instigating the systematic documentation and study of all that was found and proceeding in line with a rational excavation project. Among other things Fiorelli also devised the method of casting in plaster that made it possible to reproduce the shape of the corpses or other organic remains. Under Amedeo Maiuri, superintendent from 1924 to 1961, activity flourished, leading to the discovery of buildings of exceptional value such as the Villa of the Mysteries. Today Pompeii is a milestone in western culture and a mine of information on the ancient world that is unique of its kind. It is the duty of all of us to preserve it for future generations.

Since 1997 the Vesuvian archaeological areas have been inscribed by UNESCO in the list of World Heritage Sites.
Today the dominant problem is the conservation of the excavations, which explains why approximately one third of the 66 hectares of the ancient city have not yet been excavated.

Plaster cast of a victim.

Excavations of Herculaneum: the House of Argo, from Zuccagni-Orlandini, 1845.

Plaster cast of a victim from the House of Fabius Rufus.

17

The Forum.

① SUBURBAN BATHS

Set immediately beyond the walls, on the left of the road leading to Porta Marina, the baths were brought to light in 1985-87.

They extend over two floors; the ground floor is occupied by the baths premises while on the upper floor are residential apartments.

The baths premises consist of a changing room (*apodyterium*), a room for cold baths (*frigidarium*) with a swimming pool complete with a spectacular mosaic *nymphaeum*, a medium temperature bath room (*tepidarium*) and a room for ablutions with hot water (*calidarium*). At a later stage another three rooms were constructed around a hot water pool, the only one of such dimensions existing in Pompeii.

In the changing room, eight erotic scenes were discovered in the upper part of the south wall set above a series of progressively numbered rectangular elements resembling boxes.

The theory is that the boxes represent the wooden containers provided in the changing room for the bathers to put their clothes into, and that the erotic scenes connected with them were used in a playful manner to make it easier to replace the boxes in the correct position, which was thus identified not only by the number but also by the more easily remembered erotic position.

Suburban Baths: the baths building fits perfectly into the superb panoramic position of the site and its natural slope.

⑧③ IMPERIAL VILLA

This is an aristocratic residence of the early imperial age, built up behind the city walls on the panoramic slope stretching down towards the sea; destroyed by the earthquake of 62 AD it was never rebuilt.

Still visible are the colonnade of about 80 metres, consisting of the remains of 43 columns that stand out against the rear wall decorated with black panels bearing pictures that were brutally removed in the eighteenth century. The colonnade led to living quarters, of which there remain a large *triclinium* room, an alcove with windows overlooking the sea and other smaller rooms. The decoration of

Panel located in the upper section of the front wall of the Salone of the Imperial Villa.

the three walls is in the Third Style, with a dado surmounted by a frieze with cupids and vegetable tendrils, and the middle section coloured in Pompeii red comprising figurative pictures enclosed in *aediculae* inspired by Hellenistic models. Portrayed on the rear wall is the legend of Theseus slaying the Minotaur, while on the left is a picture of Theseus abandoning Ariadne, and on the right the flight of Daedalus and the fall of Icarus.

Imperial Villa. Theseus slaying the Minotaur, showing in the background the city of Athens and the statue of the goddess Athena.

Picture from the Imperial Villa.

The Imperial Villa seen from the south.

(2) PORTA MARINA

This was the entrance to Pompeii for those approaching from the sea, hence its name. It must have been an entrance that was fairly difficult to negotiate in view of the steep slope, although useful for linking the harbour emporium to the Forum. The gate has the appearance of a tower with two arched doorways of different dimensions, one for pedestrians and the other through which the wagons passed. This is followed by a single gallery with a barrel vault that ends in the stretch of Via Marina that flanks the Temple of Venus.

(3) TEMPLE OF VENUS

Venus was the protective deity of the city. After having conquered the city and declared it a Roman colony Sulla dedicated it to Venus, his favourite deity, so that Pompeii assumed the title *Colonia Cornelia Veneria Pompeianorum*.

The temple was built entirely of marble, clearly visible even from the sea. Today only a few remains have survived, both because of the devastation wreaked by the earthquake of 62 AD and on account of the plundering of building materials that took place after

Porta Marina.

The Temple of Venus.

the city was buried in 79 AD. The entrance to the sacred area, marked off by a high wall, was at the north-east corner on Via Marina. The temple was set upon a podium of approximately 30 metres by 15, surrounded by a colonnade with a double row of columns on the long sides and a single row to the north. The eastern side, adorned by two pedestals with statues, gave access to the houses set on the slopes of the temple terrace which were destined to the priests of Venus.

Temple of Apollo. The interior of the cella with a pavement in polychrome marble.

TEMPLE OF APOLLO

The cult of Apollo was transmitted to the Italic peoples by the Greeks. His temple in Pompeii was present from the very foundation of the city, as witnessed by the fragments of Attic and Corinthian ceramics and the remains of Etruscan pottery. During the second century BC it was rebuilt in its present form. The temple was surrounded by Corinthian columns and featured a travertine altar at the top of a high flight of steps and a solar clock on one side. In the time of Nero, after the earthquake of 62

AD, the columns and the entablature were covered with stucco, vestigial traces of which remain. The gates that linked the temple directly to the Forum were closed when the centre of worship of the city shifted to the Temple of Jupiter, and niches that are still visible were set up in their place. Set along the colonnade were a number of statues of deities that are now replaced by copies. On the right, the bronze statue of Apollo the archer and sun god, and on

the opposite side the bust of Diana, Apollo's sister and emblem of the opposing polarity, that of the moon.

The Temple of Apollo, from Zuccagni-Orlandini, 1845.

The Temple of Apollo, by V. Loria.

The Temple of Apollo: note also the solar clock on the column at the left side of the steps, a gift of the city magistrates in the imperial era.

5

BASILICA

The Basilica was built around the end of the second century BC on the western side of the Forum, with its main entrance overlooking the latter. It was in this important public building that justice was administered, as illustrated by the numerous graffiti discovered on the walls: *bassilica*, which in Greek signified the house of the king, and hence the palace of justice.

In the interior business transactions were also conducted, as in a sort of stock exchange.

The building has a rectangular layout with three aisles and a pitched roof supported by the central columns and by the semi-columns on the upper part of the walls. Ionic semi-columns were built up against the side walls, decorated with stucco in the First Style. The Basilica overlooked a loggia with large openings in the outer walls. On the side opposite the entrance, raised by about two metres and

The Basilica, from Zuccagni-Orlandini, 1845.
Top: the interior of the Basilica.

The Basilica: the remains of the interior colonnade.

set forward from the rectangular perimeter of the building, was the tribunal. Bordered at the front by six Corinthian columns, it was not connected with the main hall, and could only be accessed by using a wooden ladder. This was where the magistrate presided, in a position which guaranteed him isolation, and hence protection in the face of the frequently violent reactions of the "defendants".

The legal functions must instead have taken place in the two lateral areas, from which steps led to the crypt set beneath the podium.

The entrance from the Piazza of the Forum.

6

THE FORUM

The Forum was the centre of public life of the city and was a pedestrian area closed to the traffic of the wagons. This was where the principal civic, religious and commercial functions of the city were concentrated, and there were no private residences; overlooking the forum were the most important public buildings and several markets. Being the site of political and religious power, it changed with the different cultural and religious trends that succeeded each other in Pompeii up to 79 AD.

The architecture of the square was characterised by a colonnade with a loggia that surrounded it on three sides, leaving open the view of the Temple of Jupiter. Only slight traces of the original pavement in travertine remain. Originally the colonnade was a double order of columns made of tuff from Nocera, Doric in the lower order and Ionic on the upper level.

Some remains of these are visible

in the southern part of the Forum, while traces of the stairs that led to the loggia are also visible in the western part.

In the Julian-Claudian period work on the colonnade in travertine was begun, but never completed. The monumental bases used for equestrian statues of emperors and city notables are still visible, among them the *Suggestum*, which was used as a rostrum during the assemblies. The works undertaken to repair the damage of the earthquake of 62 AD transformed the piazza into a building site, and all the statues were moved, and in fact not a single statue has been recovered here.

The piazza was also very probably plundered following the eruption of 79 AD, and many of the precious marbles were carried off.

The two triumphal arches at the sides of the Temple of Jupiter bore equestrian statues at the summit, creating an evocative scenographic impact. The arch to the right of the temple was probably dedicated to Nero.

The Forum, from Zuccagni-Orlandini, 1845.

The colonnade on the south side of the Forum.
Below: aerial view of the Forum from the north.

The Capitolium and, in the foreground, the remains of the colonnade of the Forum.

The Forum: the Capitolium with at the sides the two triumphal arches and the profile of Vesuvius in the background.

7

MUNICIPAL BUILDINGS AND COMITIUM

Three identical buildings on the south side of the piazza housed the municipal offices.

These were the headquarters of the *duovirs*, the principal civic authority, of the *aediles*, the magistrates appointed to the maintenance of the city, and of the administrative archives.

The first building on the right, on the corner with the Basilica, was probably the Curia, appointed as the seat of the *Ordo Decurionum*, or municipal council.

This edifice, which preserves its marble pavement, has a characteristic apse at one end, while the two walls each feature three rectangular niches which housed honorary statues of emperors or of the most influential citizens of Pompeii. The central building was probably the premises of the *duovirs*. It is interesting to note the presence of small pilasters that indicate the presence of a podium to house the wooden cupboards where the administrative archives were kept.

Finally, the third building is considered to be the seat of the *aediles*. On the corner with Via dell'Abbondanza is the *Comitium* where the municipal elections were held. It originally had five entrances on the north side and five on the east, through which the voters were able to enter the Forum to vote, emerging afterwards on Via dell'Abbondanza. After the earthquake of 62 AD these entrances were reduced to three: one on the north side and two giving onto the Forum.

Statue of Holconius Rufus.

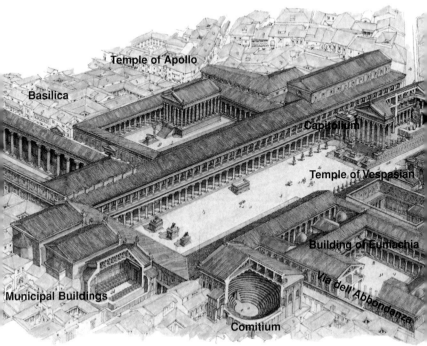

Reconstruction of the Piazza of the Forum.

THE PUBLIC ADMINISTRATION

Colonia Cornelia Veneria Pompeianorum

This was the name given to Pompeii in 80 BC after the conquest by Sulla and its reduction to a colony. The administration of the city was entrusted to four magistrates elected annually directly by the people. These consisted of a pair of *duoviri iuri dicundo*, appointed to the administration of justice, and a pair of *aediles* a who were entrusted with the care of the streets, the sacred and public buildings and the markets, as well as with law and order and the organisation of the games. Then there was a council of decurions (*ordo decurionum*), composed of a hundred former magistrates, which had powers of resolution and control over all spheres of public life, and maintained the relations with Rome. Each year when it was necessary to elect the magistrates the entire body of citizens took part in the electoral campaign. Unlike modern electoral manifestos, however, those of Pompeii, known as *programmata*, consisted not of paper documents but of exhortations written on the walls. Moreover, the electoral manifestos were not comprised in the propaganda that the candidate himself was allowed to engage in, and they were signed not by him but by friends, relatives and supporters.

The manifesto generally comprised the name of the candidate and the indication of the office he was running for, followed by the invitation to vote using the formula OFV (*oro vos faciatis*, "we ask you to elect him") and details of the particular merits of the candidate summarised in the form of abbreviations such as DRP (*dignum rei publicae* "worthy of the Republic") VB (*virum bonum*, "an honest man"). and other adjectives denoting qualities considered essential for wielding public power. Women were not entitled to vote but took an active part in the electoral campaign, promoting the candidates of their choice.

In the Samnite period the city was governed by a supreme magistrate called the *meddix tuticus*, who also appears to have been responsible for the administration of justice.

Electoral propaganda on the walls of Via dell'Abbondanza.

The marble inscription on the portico.
Left: detail of the marble frieze of the portal.

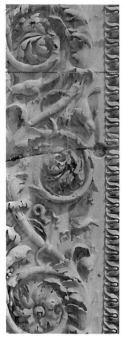

8
BUILDING OF EUMACHIA

This elegant building is situated facing the Forum, after the junction with Via dell'Abbondanza, with a fine entrance portal with marble frieze. It was the headquarters of the guild of wool and textile manufacturers. Two inscriptions, one on the marble portico of the Forum and the other on the secondary entrance of Via dell'Abbondanza, suggest that this building was dedicated to the priestess of Venus, Eumachia, who inherited from her husband a flourishing commercial activity connected with the wool industry. The building dating to the Tiberian age has a facade overlooking the Forum, moulded by two apses and four rectangular niches.

As we can deduce from the fragments of the inscriptions, these housed the statues of the ancestors of the imperial family: Aeneas, Romulus, Julius Caesar and Augustus, on the model of the Forum of Augustus in Rome.

On entering we note on the right a room used as a urinal (the urine

The entrance to the Building of Eumachia seen from the Forum.

was collected and used as a bleaching agent in the processing of the fabrics).

The internal area is characterised by a vast courtyard where we can see the remains of a colonnade with two orders of columns and an apse that housed a podium with the statue of Concordia Augusta. Beyond the wall of the portico, broken up by large windows, the *cryptoporticus* extended on three sides.

Here at the rear of the apse, the statue of Eumachia was found, set in a niche adjacent to a small corridor leading to Via dell'Abbondanza, exactly opposite the fountain that gives its name to the road.

The building, which had been damaged by the earthquake of 62 AD, was only partially restored.

The north side of the Forum. Below, the statue of Eumachia, from W. Gell, 1819.

TEMPLE OF VESPASIAN

The temple was built after 62 AD in honour of the emperor.
A central doorway leads into a space in front of the sacred area, bordered at the front by four columns. Inside, set upon a podium that can be reached by two side staircases, stood the cella where the statue of the cult was located. A marble altar decorated in bas-relief is visible in the centre of the sacred area.

Reconstruction of the Temple of Vespasian.

The altar of the temple shows a scene of sacrifice; on the opposite side is a crown of oak leaves, identical to that set at the entrance to the House of Augustus on the Palatine in Rome, and two laurel trees. The other two sides feature musical instruments and objects pertaining to the sacrificial rituals.

The Temple of Vespasian in a period photo.

Reconstruction of the Forum.

(10) SANCTUARY OF THE PUBLIC LARES

This was built by the people of Pompeii after the terrible earthquake of 62 AD and dedicated to the protective deities of the city. At the moment of the eruption it was still unfinished. It was open to the Forum via a colonnade, traces of the bases of which are still visible at the level of the colonnade of the piazza.

The sacred area was paved in polychrome marble and was open to the sky with an altar in the centre. The walls of the sanctuary featured two recessed areas at either side of the entrance and a series of niches in the masonry where the statues of other *Lares* were placed.

(11) MACELLUM

This was built in the Augustan age and was a covered market destined to the sale of meat and fish. The main entrances, thronged with stalls, were from the Forum and from Via degli Augustali, while the secondary entrance opened onto the Vico del Balcone Pensile, which was then closed for the construction of the Sanctuary of the Lares. From the Forum – divided into two paths by a votive aedicula or shrine – we enter the originally porticoed courtyard. At the rear we can observe three chambers, the central one of which was used as a chapel dedicated to the imperial family.

The chamber on the left was instead used for sacrificial banquets, while the area on the right – with a counter in masonry running the entire length and a channel for water drainage – was used for the sale of fish.

The Macellum, from W. Gell, 1819.

Situated on the north side of the Forum, with two triumphal arches at the sides and the profile of Vesuvius looming in the background, this is the icon of Pompeii. Up to the time of Sulla's conquest, this was the Temple of Jupiter. As a result of the process of Romanisation of the entire city of Pompeii that followed colonisation, the Temple of Jupiter was reno-

Above, the Triumphal Arch of Pompeii by E. Gaeta. Below, the Capitolium.

Digital reconstruction of the Capitolium by F. Russo. Below: the Capitolium.

vated and transformed into the Capitolium, dedicated to the Capitoline triad of Jupiter, Juno and Minerva, bringing it into line with the religious tradition of Rome which required every city to have a temple dedicated to the greatest deities of Olympus. The temple was set upon a high podium of the Italic type, meas-uring about 17 metes in width and 37 in length, with broad steps running along the entire length of the facade. At the top of the steps six Corinthian columns (originally about 12 metres high) led into a *pronaos* or porch in front of the cella.

The latter was divided into three areas housing the statues of the Capitoline triad.

Entrance to the temple was via two flights of steps at the sides.

(13)
GRAIN MARKET

This building is currently used as a repository for archaeological finds. Originally it opened onto the Forum and was destined to the sale of cereals, herbs and dried legumes; at the time of the eruption it was still unfinished.

⁸⁴ LATRINE

Beyond the storeroom for archaeological finds is a room leading into the latrine behind, which in Roman times was used collectively.

On the three sides of this room is the drainage channel, placed above which were seats made of masonry or wood.

The interior of the Latrine.

¹⁴ MENSA PONDERARIA

In the central part of the Forum was the Mensa Ponderaria, set within a niche carved out of the wall of the adjacent Temple of Apollo.

This was the public office that served for the control of the weights and measures used by the merchants.

It consisted of a large slab of limestone with nine circular cavities, each of a different capacity. At the base of each cavity a hole let the goods flow out under the surveillance of the officials. The mensa had been in use since the Samnite period, but from 20 BC the number of measures was increased to twelve to adapt to the parameters of the Roman system of measurement, as explained by an inscription that the *duovirs* had engraved on the new slab.

The Mensa Ponderaria: observe the cavities each corresponding to a unit of weight.
Below: plaster cast of one of the victims.

(15)
BATHS OF THE FORUM

The baths complex was built using public funds when Pompeii became a Roman colony. Following the damage of the earthquake of 62 AD these baths were immediately restored, and they were the only ones in use at the time of the eruption of 79 AD. They were not particularly large but comprised all the typical facilities of the Roman baths.

They had separate sections for men and women, with independent entrances. From Via delle Terme a narrow corridor paved with white mosaic led directly to the *apodyterium*.

This changing room, where the bathers placed their clothes in wooden cupboards, had a barrel vault and masonry benches along the sides, and was illuminated by a glass skylight with a metal frame. The walls were yellow and the ceiling was decorated in relief stucco. The *apodyteri-um* led into the *frigidarium*, or cold baths, a square chamber illuminated by an opening in the ceiling, with apsed niches at the corners and a circular marble bath with steps in the centre. The changing room also led to the *tepidarium*, another room with a barrel vault and walls elegantly decorated in stucco, where we can see niches separated from each other by the figures of giants supporting a shelf. This was the room where bathers prepared for the hot bath, and it was heated to a warm temperature using a bronze brazier. The *calidarium* was where the hot bath was located, and on the opposite side the marble *labrum* tub with cold water in which the bathers used to cool themselves. The room was heated via the circulation of hot air through an air space in the walls created using special bricks called *tegulae mammatae*. There was an analogous series of rooms in the women's section, with entrance from Via delle Terme, located beyond the boiler that served both sections of the baths.

The Tepidarium of the men's section of the Baths of the Forum. Above: the Frididarium

THE CITY OF VENUS

The oldest temples of the city were dedicated to the cult of the god Apollo and that of Minerva and Hercules.

With the foundation of the Roman colony (80 BC), the city pantheon was enriched by other deities with new temples dedicated to them. On the south-western edge of the city, the Temple of Venus was built, dedicated to the protective deity of the city, the goddess of love and fertility and protectress of sailors and maritime traffic. A temple in the Forum was dedicated to the cult of Jupiter, which later in the imperial era was transformed into a building dedicated to the Capitoline Triad (Jupiter, Juno and Minerva). In the imperial age the expansion of the cult linked to the worship of the imperial family was illustrated by the construction of the Temple of Fortuna Augusta and the Temple of Vespasian. There were also mystery cults that were practised in private confraternities and had secret rituals for the initiation of the followers. The most widespread of these was the cult of Bacchus, the god of wine and inebriation. Another mystery cult was that of the Egyptian goddess Isis, which spread through Pompeii and the rest of Campania in the second century BC. Her role as a deity who comforted human suffering made Isis greatly loved at all levels of society. Alongside this public religion there was also a highly developed private religion linked to the cult of the *Lares* and the *Panates*. The

A large phallus on a bronze pendant; the male sexual attribute was considered as a good luck amulet.

Panates were originally the gods that guarded over the foodstuff provisions (*penus*), and offerings of spelt and salt were made to them. Over time their cult became bound up with that of the *Lares*, the protective deities of the home and the family. The *Lares* were represented as youths with short fluttering tunics holding cornucopias, the symbol of abundance, and the *rhyton*, a drinking vessel in the form of a horn. Little shrines dedicated to the *Lares* (*Larari*) were generally located in the atrium of the home or close to the kitchen. Then there were also the *Lares Compitales*, who guarded crossroads and thoroughfares, and many of the altars dedicated to them are still to be seen in Pompeii.

Two "magic hands" made of bronze inspired by the god of vegetation Sabazios were discovered in one of the houses. They show hands in the act of blessing with the ring finger and little finger bent, while the palm is dominated by the figure of Sabazio himself surrounded by symbols inspired by various deities: the pine cone of Attis, the caduceus of Mercury, the cymbal and tambourine of Cybele. On the wrist is the effigy of a mother feeding an infant, testifying to the diffusion of the cult of Sabazio among new mothers.

(16)
TEMPLE OF FORTUNA AUGUSTA

The Temple stands at the cross-roads between Via del Foro and Via della Fortuna and was con-structed in the last years of the first century BC by a relative of Cicero, Marcus Tullius. The latter was an authoritative figure in Pompeii, *duovir* on a number of occasions at the time of Augustus. After having built the temple he selected the board of priests for the cult of Fortuna Augusta.

The temple consequently had a political significance which was channelled through the spread of the imperial cult, and every time that a new Emperor was pro-

A reconstruction of the Temple of Fortuna Augusta, from W. Gell, 1819.

Via della Fortuna in a period photograph.

The Temple of Fortuna Augusta and at the left the Arch of Caligula.

claimed, the ministers immediately proceeded to set up a statue to him in the temple, complete with a stone inscription. It must have been an exceptionally beautiful building, on account of both the quantity and the quality of the marble which can still be discerned in the Corinthian capitals. The building was destroyed by the earthquake of 62 BC, and was not entirely rebuilt. The layout was similar to that of the Temple of Jupiter in the Forum: the cella, set upon a high podium, was reached by a flight of steps interrupted by a small terrace on which the altar stood. In the interior of the cella, set in an *aedicula* at the rear, was the statue of Fortuna Augusta, with honorary statues in the four niches at the sides.

ARTS AND TRADES

The discovery in Pompeii of shops, working tools, pictures and inscriptions helps us to identify the activities carried out by the majority of the citizens: craftsmen, merchants, entrepreneurs and individuals that engaged in freelance activi-

ties. Many of these workers were members of guilds, such as that of the perfumiers, which had its premises on the upper floor of the *Macellum*.

The jewellers and the gem dealers have been identified through the discovery of their workshops with numerous gems and stones in different phases of working and the related tools of the trade. For the care of the person there were barbers, hairdressers and make-up experts. Other citizens of Pompeii worked as shoemakers, tanners, bronze-workers, smiths, carpenters, builders, potters, marble-workers, painters and mosaicists. There was a flourishing textile industry with numerous workshops engaged in the various phases: in the *lanificariae* the raw wool was beaten and washed, in the *textoriae* it was spun and woven and finally the resulting fabrics were dyed in the *tinctoriae*. There were also many laundries (*ful-*

lonicae) where clothes were washed, the stains removed and then bleached, using human or animal urine for the latter procedure. The *pistrina* produced bread and sweetmeats, and almost all these bakeries were provided with millstones to grind the wheat and ovens to bake the products. There were teachers who gave lessons, and the *scriptores*, professional scribes who wrote by night on the walls of the city.

Considered as infamous trades for a free citizen were those of the actor, such as Caius Norbanus Sorex — a bronze statue of whom was discovered — and of the gladiator who fought in the arena. There is also evidence of doctors and surgeons. In the Palaestra Grande and in the Amphitheatre there may have been a type of "first aid" area to treat the casualties that could arise during the gymnastic contests and possibly also those of the gladiators.

(70) VIA DI MERCURIO AND TOWER OF MERCURY

This was the residential quarter of the city par excellence where the new and old nobility resided, as reflected in the beauty and opulence of the dwellings.

Via di Mercurio owes its name to the fountain located near the House of the Small Fountain, with the pilaster surmounting the basin decorated in relief with the head of Mercury.

To the north of this area we can admire the impressive Tower of Mercury. After the third century BC, together with other towers this was encompassed into the wall circle to improve the defence of the city.

From the terrace of the tower, once complete with battlements, we can admire a view of the entire city. The interior of the tower has three floors connected by stairs, with the intermediate level linked to the parapet walk along the walls.

The Via di Mercurio with the Arch of Caligula in the foreground.

43

(17) HOUSE OF THE FAUN

The house owes its name to the bronze statuette of the dancing faun that adorned the *impluvium*. With the entrance on Via della Fortuna, this house of a surface area of three thousand square metres is the largest and most opulent private dwelling in Pompeii. This was a Samnite house, built at the beginning of the second century BC over an older one, and it has a singular architectural structure with two atria, two *peristyles*, four *triclinia* and a small baths system. The two different sections of the house develop around the two atria. The western section, with an atrium of the Tuscan order and the entrance walls decorated in the First Style, was of a residential character, while the eastern part recognisable by the tetrastyle *atrium*, was destined to service quarters.

Arranged around the main atrium are the bedrooms (*cubicula*), while at the rear on the side opposite the entrance is the *tablinum*, or reception room. In this room, featuring a pavement with perspective cubes made of palombino, slate and green limestone, a skeleton was found which may have been that of the wealthy mistress of the house, who had jewels and coins with her at the time. At the sides of the *tablinum* are the two winter *triclinia*, or dining rooms. Behind is the first *peristyle* with 28 tuff columns covered in stucco. At the end of the *peristyle* is the *exedra*, or vestibule, the threshold of which was decorated in mosaic with scenes from the Nile, divided into three sections between the entrance columns. The pavement was decorated with the magnificent mosaic

The mosaic pavement with the child Dionysius riding a tiger, by G. Abbate.

The House of the Faun, by T. Duclère.
Facing page: Via di Mercurio and in the background the Tower of the same name.

45

showing the Battle of Issus between Alexander the Great and the Persian king Darius, executed using over a million and a half tesserae. At the sides of the two summer *triclinia* that surround the *exedra* is a corridor leading to a second and larger *peristyle* with 48 Doric columns. At the end of the *peristyle* are two rooms for the gardener and two *lararium* niches, as well as a secondary entrance from Vicolo di Mercurio. In the service quarters, the entrance to which is separated from the former by two shops, we can see a number of bedrooms for the servants. In a narrow corridor leading to the *peristyle* were the kitchen, the latrine and a small baths system consisting of a *tepidarium* and *calidarium*, which utilised the heat produced by the oven in the adjacent kitchen.

The atrium of the house with the impluvium.

(18)
HOUSE OF THE LARGE FOUNTAIN AND HOUSE OF THE SMALL FOUNTAIN

The House of the Small Fountain, by G. Marsigli 1830.

At the end of the garden of this house in Via di Mercurio we can admire the beautiful large fountain decorated with polychrome mosaics and pieces of glass paste. The shells of molluscs are used to embellish the edges of the *nymphaeum*, while the original decoration is completed by two theatrical masks set into the base of the frame. The water gushed forth from the centre of the apsed recess and then fell onto the marble steps creating a singular water play before flowing into the basin beneath. Here in a fine central position is the bronze statue of a Cupid bearing a dolphin on his shoulders (now replaced by a copy).

In the next house is another fountain, again at the end of the garden, but here set between large paintings of landscapes. This fountain is decorated like the other, and the water gushed forth from a marble mask in the form of Silenus.

The House of the Small Fountain: the fountain.

The House of the Small Fountain.

(19) HOUSE OF THE DIOSCURI (HOUSE OF CASTOR AND POLLUX)

The house was created by knocking together three older houses, that can still be partially discerned. The *atrium*, with twelve columns, is one of the finest examples of a Corinthian *atrium*.
Several wall paintings, such as that of the Dioscuri in the entrance, have been moved to the Museum of Naples, but the *peristyle* that was added at a later date to the older section of the house still retains the walls largely decorated in the Fourth Style: pictures framed by slender architectures and interspersed with still lifes.

The House of the Dioscuri: a fresco showing the scene of the recognition of Achilles in Scyros.

The House of the Dioscuri: a comic scene by G. Marsigli.

A view of the interior by G. Gigante Below: the peristyle.

20
HOUSE OF MELEAGER

The house is named after a painting of Meleager with Atalanta on the left of the entrance. One of the characteristic features of this house is the elegant *oecus*, or sitting room, with Corinthian columns.

The Corinthian oecus of the House of Meleager.

The pool in the garden of the House of Meleager.

(21)
HOUSE OF APOLLO

The house takes its name from a number of paintings and a bronze statue portraying the god. The statues of Apollo and Faunus adorned the entrance to the *tablinum*. The house was elegantly decorated and the mosaic showing Ulysses recognising Achilles in disguise and concealed among the daughters of King Lycomedes of Scyrus is still visible.

The House of Apollo, the garden and the bedroom.
Below: reconstruction of the House of the Tragic Poet.

22
HOUSE OF THE TRAGIC POET

The name of this house derives from a mosaic picture showing a theatrical scene with actors and musicians. The *domus* is of the Italic type with a Tuscan style *atrium* and *peristyle* with a *lararium* at the rear.

In front of the entrance is a pavement in *cocciopesto* (lime mortar with crushed tile and ceramic fragments) adorned with large pieces of travertine, immediately followed by a mosaic portraying an aggressive dog with the legend Cave Canem: "beware of the dog". Opening onto the *atrium*, beyond the *cubicoli* is the *tablinum*. This is where the mosaic showing musicians rehearsing was found, along with several paintings inspired by the *Iliad*.

In the *triclinium*, which opens to the right of the *peristyle*, are a number of frescoes where we can note a series of paintings on mythological subjects: Ariadne abandoned by Thesues at the end of the room and, on the left wall, a nest of cupids.

The House of the Tragic Poet. Below: the House of Pansa, from Zuccagni-Orlandini, 1845.

23
HOUSE OF PANSA

This huge house, which occupies the entire *insula*, belonged to Gnaeus Alleius Nigidius Maius, a wealthy merchant who was elected as *duovir* in the year 55-56 AD.

A notice painted on the walls of an adjacent lane informs us that part of the house was rented. The building dates to the second century BC, as we can deduce from the Ionic capitals in the garden colonnade.

24
HOUSE OF THE BAKERY

This building, which was transformed into a bakery after the renovation that followed the earthquake of 62 AD, stands on the corner between Via Consolare and Via di Mercurio, and the conversion had not been completed at the time of the eruption. The remains of a mule used to turn the grindstones were found in the stable.

25
HOUSE OF SALLUST

This house dates to the third century BC and is one of the oldest in the city; it suffered serious damage in the bombardment of 1943. The house had been transformed into a restaurant and hotel, with the bedrooms on the upper floor. It is arranged with the rooms around the *atrium*, and behind the *tablinum* is a small portico with a garden and a summer *triclinium* with masonry couches.

A bakery, from Zuccagni-Orlandini, 1845.

At the rear of the building are a kitchen, dining room and bedrooms. On the street front are four shops, a tavern, a bakery with three millstones and an oven complete with fireplace.

The House of Sallust, the atrium.

THE EATING HABITS OF THE ROMANS

Roman cuisine was originally very simple and almost exclusively vegetarian. The most widespread comestible meat was pork, which was also dried so that it would keep for longer. The Romans consumed pulses too, often combined with a sort of polenta called *puls*, made from spelt cooked in water and salt. Bread was an important foodstuff, and originally the bread was baked at home, but from the second century BC on the custom of purchasing it in special shops, known as the *pistrina*, became widespread. After the conquest of Greece the consumption of meat increased, as well as that of game and many types of birds, which were reared in special aviaries for the purpose. Among the birds that were bred were thrushes, pheasants, guinea-fowl and even storks and cranes. Dormice too, which were considered a delicacy, were bred in special clay containers called *gliraria*. The consumption of fish also increased, the most appreciated species being eels, dorado, sole, mullet, turbot, sturgeon, moray, oysters and crustaceans. The most characteristic element of Roman cooking was *garum*, a pungent sauce made from minced fish entrails that was used to flavour a great many dishes. There were a variety of types, more or less appreciated depending on the quality of the fish used and the method of preparation. The *garum* produced in Pompeii was particularly prized. Fruit was always present on the tables of the Romans, in particular figs, grapes, peaches, apples and pomegranates, which we also frequently find illustrated in the paintings of Pompeii.

The Romans were great lovers of sweetmeats, and of ice-creams which they made with white flour tempered in sweet wine and snow. Another distinctive feature was the considerable use of condiments and aromatic herbs. A cornerstone of Roman cuisine has come down to us in the form of the famous "De re coquinaria" cookery book by the gastronomist Marcus Gavius Apicius who lived at the time of Tiberius. This collection of recipes, combined with the archaeological discoveries and the information handed down by the Latin writers (Pliny, Juvenal, Martial, Petronius etc.) has enabled us to acquire a detailed knowledge of many aspects of Roman cuisine, especially that of the imperial period when the foodstuffs cast off the frugality of the Republican era and adopted the fashions of imperial opulence. Apicius was in fact not only a master of the culinary

Eggs and fowl, from the Praedia of Julia Felix.

arts but also an extravagant eccentric.

Two modernised recipes from the "De re coquinaria"

Starter with apricots.

Peel 700 g of apricots, cut and stone them and put them in a pan with cold water.

Grind 7 pepper corns and add 1 spoon of dried mint, then mix with 5 spoons of garum sauce, add a spoonful of honey, half a glass of Muscat from Pantelleria, half a glass of dry Marsala and 1 spoon of vinegar.

Pour over the apricots and trickle over a little oil; cook over a low heat without a lid for half an hour. Drain the cooking juices into a recipient, add two spoons of corn starch and beat until smooth, then pour over the apricots again. Cook until the sauce has thickened and then serve hot or warm garnished with a sprinkle of ground pepper.

Boiled duck with pine kernels and dates.

Cut the duck into sections, removing the fat and the

Cooking utensils in bronze and lead, by V. Loria.

backbone, breastbone and neck bone. Place in a large flat pan. Chop 6 peppercorns, the same of ligustrum (privet), a pinch of cumin, 1 spoon of coriander, 1 spoon of dried mint, 1 spoon of oregano, 25 g of pine kernels, 2 large dates and 1 spoon of mustard seeds. Mix with 3 spoonfuls of soy sauce, 3 of garum, a spoonful of oil, a heaped spoonful of honey, 1 full glass of dry Marsala, 1 spoonful of vinegar and a pinch of salt. Pour over the meat, add water almost to cover. Cook slowly, stirring from time to time, until the sauce has thickened.

Bowls with fruit.

26
HOUSE OF THE SURGEON

Inside this building 40 surgical instruments were discovered, contained in metal cases.

The house is of the Italic type, and is one of the oldest in Pompeii, dating to the third century BC, even though it was renovated on various occasions, comprising the addition of an upper storey in the quarters devoted to agricultural produce.

27
PORTA ERCOLANO AND THE WALL CIRCLE

All the commercial traffic heading in the direction of Naples passed through this important city gate. It was also known as *Porta Salis*, the Salt Gate, in view of the presence of the "Saline d'Ercole" salt pits on the nearby coast. It was built following the conquest by Sulla in 89 BC.

In the stretch of walls between Porta Ercolano and Porta Vesuvio the traces left by the artillery of Sulla during the siege of 89 BC are still visible.

Porta Ercolano, from Zuccagni-Orlandini, 1845.

Digital reconstruction of Porta Ercolano, by F. Russo.

ALONG THE WALLS

It is possible to visit Pompeii via a particularly suggestive itinerary along the walls of the city, extending for approximately 3 kilometres following the perimeter of the ancient city from Porta Ercolano to Porta Nocera. This route offers panoramic views from above of the entire city and surrounding territory and a vantage point that is both unusual and little frequented by visitors.

The walls of Pompeii in a period print.

A stretch of the northern part of the walls with the remains of a tower.

The Tower of Mercury seen from the itinerary along the walls.

THE WALLS

The first wall circle of modest dimensions, encircling an area of approximately 66 hectares, was built of blocks of soft lava stone in the first half of the sixth century BC. At the beginning of the fifth century, with a technique of Greek inspiration and using large slabs of limestone, the people of Pompeii built a new "double curtain" fortification (two parallel walls with the space between filled with earth and rocks), which followed the route of the previous walls.

Towards the end of the fourth century BC, at the time of the Samnite wars, the city adopted fortifications of the Italic "ad aggere" type (that is with a reinforcement embankment on the inner side). Towards the end of the third century, to tackle the threat of Hannibal's Carthaginian army, the fortification with inner embankment was strengthened and raised to a greater height.

The last modification that the citizens of Pompeii made to the walls was the insertion of twelve watchtowers, which enhanced their defensive power. This time the danger came from Rome, against which Pompeii had rebelled taking part in the revolt of the other Italic peoples. The walls of Pompeii had their baptism of fire in 89 BC when Sulla at the command of the Roman legions laid siege to the city. The Romans concentrated their attack in the northern stretch of the walls, which in view of the lay of the land was the most vulnerable part, and the city was rapidly forced to surrender; in this stretch the signs of the damage caused by the Roman artillery are still visible.

After Pompeii became a Roman colony, the walls progressively lost their importance and function, and in the imperial age some parts of them were actually incorporated into private constructions.

View of the city from the walls.

View of the walls with modern Pompeii in the background.

(28)
THE NECROPOLIS OF PORTA ERCOLANO

Between the conquest of Sulla and the burial of the city, numerous tombs were built along Via dei Sepolcri as was the custom at the time.

These funerary monuments are of various types: *aedicula* tombs, others in the form of *exedra*, with an enclosure and an altar set upon a podium.

Yet others are of a monumental style with seats for the relatives of the deceased, such as that of Marcus Cerrinus Restitutus.

The Necropolis of Porta Ercolano by W. Day, 1830

The Necropolis of Porta Ercolano, from Zuccagni-Orlandini, 1845.

(29)
VILLA OF DIOMEDES

This is a luxury villa set on Via dei Sepolcri, with the entrance leading directly into the *peristyle* of 14 columns. In a triangular area between the road and the *peristyle* were the baths, while on the opposite side was the *triclinium* with a spectacular view over the Gulf of Naples and the vast garden beneath. In the centre of the garden was another open *triclinium* and a swimming pool, and it was bordered by a covered gallery (*cryptoporticus*) in which between 1771 and 1774 the remains of 14 victims were discovered. These included bejewelled women, children and the owner of the villa himself, with a gold ring on his finger, a silver key in his hand and 1356 *sesterces*.

The Villa of Diomedes: the peristyle.
Below: a reconstruction by J. L. Desprez.

Villa of the Mysteries, pictorial detail from the triclinium.

VILLA OF THE MYSTERIES

Situated outside the walls of the city, about 300 metres from Porta Ercolana, this the most famous and intriguing of all the villas in Pompeii. Built in the second century BC it was renovated on two occasions, in 60 BC and in the first century AD. The building consists of two sections, the residential area and the quarters devoted to agricultural produce. The first, facing the sea, features magnificent decorations in the Second and Third Styles. In the agricultural area, set to the right of the main entrance, a press for squeezing the grapes was found with a trunk in the form of a ram's head, which was discovered in the rooms used for the production of wine. On the side opposite the *peristyle*

Reconstruction of the Villa of the Mysteries, from Maiuri – Pane. Below: the peristyle.

Villa of the Mysteries: the triclinium.

Detail of the pictorial sequence.

atrium with four columns where there were also a number of small rooms with decorations in the Second Style, including a *cubiculum* with two beds (a double alcove). The *tablinum* is decorated in the Third Style on a black ground with Egyptian-style miniatures. The *tablinum* then leads into a *cubiculum* which originally had an alcove, but was later transformed into a room of passage.

The decorations are in imitation marble superimposed with panel-type paintings showing sacrificial scenes and a painting of Dionysius with a satyr and dancing maenads. These subjects, together with the paintings of sculptures of a dancing satyr, the muse Calliope and Silenus attended by a servant, appropriately set the scene for entrance to the "*triclinium* of the mysteries". The latter, like almost the entire residential quarters, stands above a three-sided *crypto-porticus* designed to compensate the natural slope of the terrain.

are the kitchens, two ovens in the courtyard, the *lararium* and a spacious latrine. Beyond the kitchen courtyard were other areas appointed as a bathroom, used as such in the pre-Roman period and later transformed into a storeroom. These opened off a small

The Paintings of the Mysteries

The walls of the *triclinium* present one of the marvels of Pompeii: an almost life size painting (megalographia) portraying a mysterious ritual which gives its name to the villa. The pictorial cycle reproduced on the walls is very probably a copy of a Greek original that has been lost, and is impressive both in terms of its majestic dimensions (17 metres long by 3 metres in height) and for its immediate and engaging visual impact. The mystical dimension is finely evoked by the artist in the expressions, glances and movements of the various figures: the multitude of symbolic references accentuates the cryptic fascination of the pictorial sequence and hints at meanings and references that for us continue to be elusive and mysterious. We should recall that the cult of Dionysius was prohibited by the Senate of Rome on account of the excesses and disorder that followed the "bacchanals".

The first scene of the pictorial sequence.

Female figures and a Satyr with musical instrument.

Details of the pictorial sequence.

PAINTING AND THE FOUR STYLES

The houses of Pompeii represent the most important documentation of Roman painting from the beginning of the second century BC to 79 AD, and only an exceptional event such as the eruption of Vesuvius has enabled such fragile and delicate materials to be preserved. The fashion for decorating the walls with painting was common among all the people who could afford it. The decorators proceeded to the execution of the decorative scheme of the wall, with the exception of the central panel, which was then entrusted to a more skilled artist, known as the *pictor imaginarius*. Before the painting, the wall was prepared with several layers of lime and sand mortar (and last of all a coating of marble powder) upon which the actual colour was then spread.

The wall painting was executed "*a fresco*": the colours had to be applied to the plaster before it dried, and the painter addressed a limited portion at a time, more precisely the area that it was possible to paint in one day. The pigments were normally of mineral origin, a characteristic that enabled them to be mixed with the lime without them being altered.

The yellows, reds, browns and certain greens were obtained by the decanting – and at times calcination – of different types of natural earth. The black was often obtained from soot, from bone or from wood, while the varieties of white were based on calcium carbonate. Roman wall painting has been divided into four styles.

The **First Style**, or structural style, is of Hellenistic origin and is found in Pompeii from the second century BC to the beginning of the first century BC. It consists of a stucco imitation of the marble wall covering. The stucco is also painted in bright colours to resemble the colours of the different varieties of marble.

The **Second Style**, developed in Pompeii probably under the influence of Roman colonisation (80 BC). Arches and windows painted in the upper section of the wall open up to reveal an array of architectural elements such as temples, colonnades, walls and gardens arranged on different planes (and not always following a precise perspective logic). These elements are conceived as if they are beyond the room itself, in a symbolic expansion of the space beyond the wall, which opens up the interior in what is a sort of precursor of trompe l'oeil.

Within the Second Style another specific genre evolved which was called *megalographia*. These are paintings with figures of very large dimensions, and the most famous example of these particularly elegant pictorial cycles comes from the *triclinium* of the Villa of the Mysteries.

An example of the First Style, or structural style, from the House of Sallust.

Cubiculum, or bedroom, in Second Style in the House of the Mysteries.

The **Third Style** characterised the entire early imperial age (45/50 AD). Here the illusionist element completely disappears and the wall is divided into three sections: the dado, the middle section and the upper section. The middle section in particular is characterised by a central panel, often in the form of an *aedicula*, featuring a figurative composition, generally on a mythological theme. At the sides of the *aedicula* are large panels bordered by slender architectural elements, in the centre of which are vignettes or scenes of landscape. Sometimes between the dado and the middle section there is a figured band (*predella*) and occasionally even a second band between the middle and upper areas. In the upper section slender architectural elements are accompanied by tendrils and garlands.

Third Style from the House of Marcus Lucretius Fronto.

The **Fourth Style** made its appearance in the Claudian Age, but became completely consolidated with the major restoration works that followed the earthquake of 62 AD.

The decorative sobriety of the Third Style is replaced by the Baroque and scenographic exuberance of this new mode of painting. On the wall, still strictly divided into three parts, the middle section features an alternation of large panels and architectural motifs in which the taste for articulated and superimposed perspectives resurfaces. The central panel continues to be the site of the my-

Wall in the Fourth Style showing Hercules with a female figure, from Niccolini.

67

thological painting, while in the centre of the side panels are small paintings (landscapes or still lifes) or flying figures of Cupids, portrayals of the seasons etc. The upper section, divided into architectural *aediculae* linked by tendrils, garlands and carpet fringes, is often crowned by a stucco cornice with lotus flowers and palmettes.

The tones of the colours are warmer and more brilliant and the colour effect is accentuated by the juxtaposition of large background areas of yellow, black, red or sky blue.

Another strand of the Fourth Style is that known as the *scenae frontes*, where the entire wall is covered with complex and elaborate architecture deriving from theatrical scenery, with full-size figures in the fo-

reground. There was also another type of painting in Pompeii, defined as "popular" with an independent character that can be traced to the Italic artistic world.

These tend to be paintings of the *Lares*, shop signs with illustrations of the arts and trades, erotic scenes, tavern scenes and images of gladiators. Even through the technique used

Garden painting. Orpheus among the animals from the House of Orpheus.

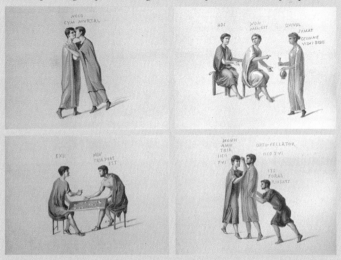

Popular paintings with tavern scenes.

proves to be of fairly poor quality, they nevertheless represent invaluable evidence of the daily life of the city.

Wall in Second Style from Oplontis.

Wall with stucco and fresco in the Fourth Style, from the Stabian Baths.

31

NECROPOLIS OF PORTA VESUVIO AND TOMB OF VESTORIUS PRISCUS

Several tombs have been found outside the walls, in the vicinity of Porta Vesuvio.

Dominating this necropolis is the tomb of the *aedile* Caius Vestorius Priscus, who died at the age of 22. An inscription records that the tomb was built on the land granted by the *decurions*, who also provided the sum of two thousand *sesterces* required for the funeral. The Tomb of Vestorius Priscus is surrounded by a high wall, with a central altar set upon a substructure containing the sepulchral chamber. It is frescoed all over with scenes of hunting, gladiator contests and silver vessels. On the southern side of the base of the altar is a portrait of the deceased in the act of administering justice.

Porta Vesuvio, on the right the Tomb of Vestorius Priscus.

(32)
CASTELLUM AQUAE

This is a work of hydraulic engineering designed to supply water to the public and private utilities of the city by collecting in the interior the water coming from a branch of the Augustan aqueduct of Serino, and dividing and regulating the flow. The introduction of this device marked a turning-point in the domestic habits of the citizens of Pompeii who had previously used the water from the wells, or from the basins for the collection of rainwater located in the *impluvia* of the houses.

Above left: a digital reconstruction of the Castellum Aquae by F. Russo
Below left: the Castellum Aquae at Porta Vesuvio. This was where the water flow was divided into three conduits to supply public fountains, baths and private dwellings respectively.

HOUSE OF THE GOLDEN CUPIDS

This is the house that belonged to the Gens Poppaea, the family of Nero's second wife. The entrance is from Via Vesuvio and it takes its name from the original decoration of the *cubiculum* which is near the shrine of the *Lares*. Discovered set into the plaster of this room were a number of glass discs covered on the rear with gold leaf and engraved with cupids. The house features an atrium with *tablinum* somewhat off-centre from the rest of the dwelling, which is arranged elegantly around the *peristyle* with garden. The portico – along which is the *lararium*, and, in a corner, the small chapel dedicated to the Egyptian triad of Harpocrates, Isis and Serapides – follows a natural slope and the western section is raised.

The House of the Golden Cupids: the cubiculum or bedroom where the cupids were found. Below: the peristyle

Located in this part are the *triclinium* with masonry couches and another two rooms: in that on the left, with a vegetable garden behind it, the seasons are shown painted on a white ground, while the other (with the kitchen behind it) features decorations on amorous themes, such as Leda and the Swan, Venus fishing, and Actaeon spying on Diana bathing. The two rooms, with coffered ceilings, convey an extremely sophisticated atmosphere.

34 HOUSE OF CAECILIUS JUCUNDUS

This house, in Via del Vesuvio, belonged to the Pompeii banker Lucius Caecilius Jucundus.
The excavations have yielded 154 wax tablets from his archives dated between 52 and 62 AD which record the sums paid to those for whom he had sold goods (above all slaves) or collected rents. Also recorded is the commission, ranging between 1% and 4% that he withheld for his action as middleman. A bronze portrait of the banker has also come down to us, which was discovered in the *tablinum*. Of particular interest

Bronze portrait of an ancestor of Caecilius Jucundus.

are the two marble reliefs (one of them subsequently stolen) that adorned the *lararium*. The reliefs show the Temple of Jupiter damaged by the earthquake of 62 AD with the sacrifice of expiation, and the Castellum Aquae with the Porta Vesuvio collapsing.

35 CENTRAL BATHS

After the earthquake of 62 AD work began on the construction of these baths. The project did not envisage separate quarters for men and women, and at the time of the eruption only the furnaces, the *palaestra*, or gymnasium, and the swimming pool were lacking.
The importance of the building is illustrated by the size of the site, which extended over an entire *insula*.

The Central Baths.

HOUSE OF MARCUS LUCRETIUS FRONTO

The house stands in the road of the same name that intersects Via di Nola, and features elegant decorations in the Third Style. The shiny black of the walls is broken up by yellow bands with arabesques and hunting scenes; the floor in black lavapesto (made of ground lava bound with sand and lime) is scattered with fragments of marble. The extremely elegant *tablinum* has landscape views of villas and gardens, and two mythological paintings: the marriage of Venus and Mars on the left wall and on the right, the Triumph of Bacchus, accompanied by Ariadne on a chariot drawn by oxen. To the right of the *tablinum*, in a room painted yellow, amidst a series of cupids is a painting showing Narcissus gazing at his reflection in the water, and on the right Perona breastfeeding her old father, Myconis. Immediately after the vestibule is the winter *triclinium*, with an illustration of a scene taken from Euripides' tragedy *Andromache*, in which Neoptolemus is killed by the sword of Orestes on the altar of Apollo. In the next *cubiculum* there is a 'triumph' of extremely small and intricate details set against a black background, while on the right wall there is a painting of Ariadne bringing Theseus the thread so that he can find his way through the labyrinth. The house has a gar-

The House of Marcus Lucretius Fronto. Above: the wall of the tablinum. Below: the atrium.

den at the back, the walls of which were painted with hunting scenes.

(36) HOUSE OF THE VETTII

This luxurious residence was excavated in 1894 and provided with a roof to protect its precious Fourth Style decorations. The excellent state of conservation of the paintings is also due to the fact that the house was restored after the earthquake of 62 AD. The excavations have brought to light numerous sculptures and marble and bronze objects which it was decided to leave in situ in view of the excellent state of conservation of the house. The owners were the Vettii, a fam-

ily of freedmen that belonged to the up and coming class which, from the Age of Augustus on and particularly after the earthquake of 62 AD, came to play an increasingly prominent role in the city. The house is divided into two areas: the part in which the family lived, laid out around the main *atrium* and the *peristyle* with its choreographic garden, and the service quarters on the right of the entrance hall and centred around a small atrium with a *lararium*. In the entrance, the right wall is decorated with a painting of Priapus weighing his enormous phallus on a pair of scales, with a bag filled with coins in the other pan. This painting had the function of warding off evil and call-

ing down prosperity upon the inhabitants of the house. The *atrium* is decorated with scenes depicting sacrifices, hunts and cupids. Fixed to a masonry block are two safes which, in view of the unusual location, were probably intended to underscore the wealth of the family for the benefit of visitors. Numerous rooms open off the *atrium*. The *cubiculum* on the left has a dado of panels of imitation marble and paintings in the central section showing the myth of Leander swimming towards his beloved Hero, while the opposite wall portrays Ariadne abandoned by Theseus on Naxos. The *oecus*, or drawing room is decorated with frescoes depicting the struggle be-

The Casa dei Vettii. Above: frieze showing cupids washing clothes.

The Casa dei Vettii: the frescoes of the oecus. Above: frieze with goldsmith cupids.

tween Cupid and Pan, and Cyparissus who was transformed into a cypress tree after accidentally stabbing to death Apollo's favourite deer, and finally several images of Jupiter in the upper section of the wall. To the west of the *atrium*, in the two *alae* before coming to the garden, we can see on the left a scene of cock-fighting and on the right two medallions with the heads of Medusa and Silenus. On the eastern side is a staircase leading to the upper floor, and opposite is a sumptuous *lararium*. After this comes the kitchen, where a number of bronze saucepans were found. In the residential section of the house, the *peristyle* surrounds an elegant garden that has been reconstructed following the original layout. Here we find a lavish decorative apparatus consisting of statues of cupids and cherubs in marble and bronze, columns decorated with herms, and tables. On the four sides are rectangular marble fountains, while

at the corners and in the middle are other fountains, circular in shape. The reception rooms facing onto the *peristyle* are most beautiful and evocative, with a wealth of paintings on mythological subjects set inside painted *aediculae*. The living room on the left just beyond the atrium has walls with a yellow ground painted with frescoes depicting, on the left the child Hercules strangling the serpents sent by Juno, and on the right, the punishment of Dirce bound by her sons Amphion and Zetus to the horns of a raging bull; in the centre is the scene of the torture of Pentheus, stoned by the Bacchantes. On the opposite side is a magnificent reception room with three large paintings. On the left is Daedalus presenting Pasiphae with the wooden cow in which she was to conceal herself since she had become enamoured of a bull, as a result of which union she was to give birth to the Minotaur. The central painting shows the punish-

ment inflicted on Ixion who is tied to a wheel built by Hephaestus and made to turn for all eternity, in the presence of Hera sitting on the throne, and Hermes. On the right is Bacchus watching Ariadne as she sleeps upon a tiger's skin. Along the perimeter are a number of secluded rooms, which are believed to have been reserved for women (*gynaeceum*), where opposite a small garden we can see a *triclinium* and a *cubiculum*. Two frescoes preserved in this area show Achilles being recognised by Ulysses and Auge surprised by the drunken Hercules. In the centre of the north side of the colonnade is the large *triclinium* that has preserved an extremely unusual miniaturised decoration set above the dado, showing cupids and their female equivalents (*psyches*) engaged in a number of different activities. The paintings, which in this case were fastened to the wall with nails, are now missing, but on the side panels painted in cinnabar red we can

Painting with theatrical mask, and goats and asparagus.

Painting showing a cock fight, from the atrium.

lived. In the small atrium is the *lararium*, the shrine to the domestic deities, with a painting of the Genius with two dancing *Lares* at the sides above a serpent, a powerful symbol of fertility. On the hob in the kitchen we can see a number of tripods, 5 bronze saucepans and other vessels, while in the adjacent room, reserved for the cook and decorated with three erotic pictures, is the marble statue of Priapus which was originally used in the garden as a fountain.

see famous divine couples in flight: Perseus and Andromeda, Dionysus and Ariadne, Apollo and Daphne, Neptune and Amymone and Silenus astonished by Hermaphroditos.

Leaving the family section of the house, through a doorway beyond the main entrance, we reach the service quarters of a rural type, where the servants worked and

The House of the Vettii, by V. Loria.

(37) HOUSE OF THE ANCIENT HUNT

Situated on Via della Fortuna, this house is named after a magnificent wall painting in the garden with a mountain landscape and ancient scenes of hunting. It is a house of Samnite origin, with decorations in the Fourth Style. On the walls of the *atrium* are personifications of autumn and winter. In the second *cubiculum* on the right, instead, the walls are decorated with mythological subjects: on the left, Leda and the Swan, portrayed between medallions with the busts of Diana and Jupiter, and on the right, Venus fishing between Mercury and Apollo. In the *tablinum* are Nile landscapes with Pygmies, cupids hunting wild beasts, and carpets and strips of cloth billowing in the wind. In the *exedra* opposite the garden we find fantastic architectures and lavish ornamental motifs, and in the midst Diana bathing being observed by Actaeon, and Apollo in the background with a shepherd.

The hunting scenes that give its name to the House of the Ancient Hunt.
Facing page: House of the Vettii, the peristyle.

(38) BAKERY (PISTRINUM)

In the second century BC bread making at family level was almost completely replaced by industrial production. As a result about thirty different bakeries sprang up in Pompeii, like this one that belonged to Popidus Priscus.
The bakery looked onto Vicolo Storto, and does not appear to have had a sales counter, so that distribution must have been on a wholesale basis. The bakery worked with four large millstones and one small, all of them operated by mules. The millstones were composed of a fixed lower section of a conical shape (meta) and a moveable upper section in the form of a double cone, hollow inside (catillus). A rod was inserted into the narrow neck of the *catillus* which could then be turned by human or animal power. In this way the grain, which was poured into the upper cavity of the *catillus*, was ground in the lower section and emerged as flour on the circular base beneath.

Carbonised bread in the characteristic shape marked into wedges.

Fresco showing the sale of bread, from the tablinum of the House of the Baker.

(39) LUPANAR

This building, located on the corner of two secondary streets and not far from the Forum and the Stabian Baths, was the official brothel of Pompeii.

Phalluses engraved on the basalt road surface or on the facades of houses provided clear indications on how to reach the brothel. This building was explicitly indicated as a brothel, unlike other premises used for prostitution that were located on the first floors or in the back rooms of hostelries and taverns.

The tariffs for erotic services ranged from 2 to 16 asses.

The *lupanar* had five bedrooms on the ground floor and 5 larger rooms on the first floor which could be reached by an independent entrance and a wooden staircase; each bedroom had a masonry couch on which the mattress was placed.

On the wall to the right of the ground-floor entrance is a paint-

The exterior of the Lupanar.

ing of Priapus holding his two phalluses in his hands, while the doors of the bedrooms have paintings all featuring different scenes of lovemaking in various positions.

On the walls approximately 120 graffiti were discovered, featuring the comments and suggestions of the clientele.

The manager of the brothel and the owner of the prostitutes was the "*lenone*".

A bedroom with a masonry couch.

Below: paintings with erotic scenes.

EROS IN POMPEII

In Pompeii a number of paintings have been discovered illustrating explicit sexual acts, in addition to statuettes portraying mythological figures with huge phalluses, lanterns, small bronzes and marbles with erotic decorations, and representations of phalluses in bronze, terracotta, marble and paint. This does not mean that Pompeii was a dissolute city, but simply indicates that the Romans had a concept of sexuality and morality that was quite different from ours, less conditioned by the idea of sin and of prohibition.

ing the fact that such images were utilised in quite distinct contexts. The degree of familiarity that the ancients had with sexually explicit images also derives from the religious and apotropaic significance that these had. Many of them were illustrations of deities that expressed their power of fecundation by flaunting an erect penis (ithyphallic). The phallus played an important symbolic role in certain religious rituals, in particular in those connected with the cult of Dionysius. Priapus too, another god of fertility, was a

of enhancing the harvest. There are also pictures showing the god Pan pouring oil over his phallus, or images like the famous fresco from the House of the Vettii, where the deity is shown weighing his member on the pan of a scales. The phallus portrayed in isolation is an amulet used to ward off evil and as a protection against all that can threaten the happiness of the individual and his family. In Pompeii there are innumerable objects of all kinds on which the phallus is reproduced as a lucky charm:

portable amulets, sculptures, paintings used to decorate houses, shops and streets and even the paving stones.

Erotic images circulated freely on a wide variety of objects of everyday use: lamps, vessels, elegant crockery, gems and mirrors, the latter almost exclusively for female use. Hence we can see that the relationship that the Romans had with sexuality and its representations was very different

Erotic illustrations were used to decorate both sites of pleasure, such as the *Lupanar*, and the homes of the wealthy citizens of Pompeii, demonstrat-

phallic deity. He is frequently shown with his garments raised to display his sexual organ and his gown filled with fruit, an allusion to his power

from our own: sex was seen as a pleasant and indispensable component of life and as such was experienced and freely portrayed.

STABIAN BATHS

Opening onto Via dell'Abbondanza, at the corner with Via Stabiana are the oldest baths in the city. The original nucleus dates to the fourth century, and the structure was transformed into a public baths with separate sections for men and women in the second century BC.

Further additions and renovations were carried out in the colonial age (80-70 BC).

The original layout, which already comprised the central courtyard with colonnade and the *palaestra*, or gymnasium, was extended through the addition of the room for *sudationes* and the area for washing after exercise in the *palaestra*. Damaged by the earthquake of 62 AD, the building had been only partially restored at the time of the eruption. The establishment covers a total surface area of over 3,500 square metres.

The male and female sections were served by a single heating system, located between the two. The main entrance on Via dell'Abbondanza led into a large courtyard which was used as a gymnasium. This had a colonnade on three sides while on the fourth side was a large cold-water swimming pool, built around the mid first century BC. At the sides of the swimming pool are two areas with fountains, probably used as changing rooms and for washing prior to entering the swimming pool. The decoration of the swimming pool area was executed after the earthquake of 62 AD, with elegant polychrome stuccoes showing architectural perspectives and painted panels showing mythological figures and athletes (Jupiter with the sceptre and eagle, a Satyr offering drink to the drunken Hercules, wrestlers scraping themselves clean using the *strigil*).

The *palaestra* was equipped only with a number of bathrooms on the northern side and other rooms where a large latrine was later discovered.

A door in the right-hand corner of the colonnade leads to the men's section, where the first room on the left is a chamber for the cold bath (*frigidarium*). The *frigidarium* of the Stabian baths was circular in shape, with a large pool in the centre and four niches at the corners. The water used to feed the pool flowed from another niche in the north wall.

The fact that this chamber precedes the changing room suggests that it may originally have been used as a *laconicum*, a room destined to steam baths (sauna) in which the air was heated by means of bronze braziers. From the entrance hall we enter the changing room (*apodyterium*),

The Stabian Baths.

which has masonry benches along the walls for waiting or for ease of changing, and masonry niches for the garments to be placed in. The ceiling and the lunette of this chamber feature a lavish decoration in polychrome stucco. After this, on the left, is the *tepidarium*, in which warm baths were taken. It was heated by hot air which circulated under the floor (raised by small terracotta pilasters called *suspensurae*) and through cavities in the walls themselves, as we can see in various areas that were involved in the works in progress at the time of the eruption. We then move into the *calidarium*, with on the right side the rectangular pool used for the hot baths, with three niches above that contained statues. On the apsed side is the marble basin that contained cold

water used for cooling off in this particularly hot chamber. Beyond the wall of the *calidarium* were the furnaces used to heat both the water and the bath chambers of both sections.

Retracing our steps along the gymnasium colonnade, moving northwards we come to the entrance to the women's section,

with access from the Vicolo del Lupanare. Here the rooms follow the same sequence as in the men's section, but without the *frigidarium*, so that the changing room leads directly into the semi-heated room and from there to the *calidarium*, which was also equipped with bronze vessels for individual baths.

The Stabian Baths: the apodyterium.

The inner courtyard of the Stabian Baths, used as a palaestra, or gymnasium.

(41) (42)
TRIANGULAR FORUM
DORIC TEMPLE

This broad area, which assumes a triangular form to adapt to the lava spur on which it stands, was occupied since the fourth century BC by a Doric Temple.
In the second half of the second century BC the area was embellished by the construction of a colonnade and comprised within a harmonious urban design in view of the presence of the nearby theatres. The entrance to the Triangular Forum is via a vestibule preceded by a portal with three Ionic columns and a semi-col-

The Doric Temple: well with the remains of the circular building with Doric columns.

The Triangular Forum: a reconstruction. Below: a period photo.
Facing page: a reconstruction of the southern side of the city.

umn. Inside, the space is bordered by a colonnade of 95 Doric columns, except on the south side so as not to obstruct the view. Along the east side of the colonnade is a broad corridor, possibly a track for athletics or horse races. Another two passages lead to the district of the theatres. At the end of the sacred area stands the Doric Temple dedicated to Hercules, and later also to Minerva, as suggested by an Oscan epigraph discovered in the vicinity of the temple and the antefixes that decorated it. Hercules and Minerva were two deities that were highly venerated by the Italic peoples.

Renovated on several occasions, the temple was badly damaged by the earthquake of 62 BC and had been abandoned prior to the eruption. All that now survives are the substructure, a few capitals and a pedestal set off-centre on the eastern side of the cella, which was possibly matched by another on the opposite side. After the abandonment of the temple, the sacred area was used for games and athletic displays, and as an area that the public could use during intervals in the performances held in the nearby theatres.

(43) LARGE THEATRE

Despite being the only theatre in Pompeii, it was given this name to distinguish it from the nearby Odeion. It was built in the second century BC on the Greek model with the tiered seats adapted to the natural slope of the terrain and the orchestra arranged in a horse-shoe shape.

In the Augustan Age, expansion works were financed by the Holconius brothers, and there is an inscription that specified the works that were carried out: the entire seating area was resurfaced in marble – although this was subsequently plundered after the city was buried – the upper gallery was added and the two side boxes (situated above the entrance to the orchestra) were added for the guests of honour. The theatre could hold 5,000 people, seated in three different areas separated by corridors.

The first area (called the *ima cavea*) was situated in the orches-

The Large Theatre, from Zuccagni-Orlandini, 1845.

tra itself and had four rows of seats which were reserved for the *decurions*, while the first rows of the media *cavea* were for the representatives of the guilds, including the seat reserved for the eldest of the Holconius brothers with an inscription in bronze letters. The highest tiers (summa *cavea*) were designated for the ordinary people. The top tier was fitted with stone rings that were used to support the poles which held the large canopy to protect the audience from the sun.

The stage built of masonry was re-

constructed after the earthquake of 62 AD to imitate the facade of an important building decorated with columns, niches and statues.

(44) QUADRIPORTICUS OF THE THEATRES

This is a quadriporticus made up of 74 Doric columns bordering a spacious courtyard. In the last years of Pompeii it was the headquarters of the organisation of the gladiators that performed in the city. Lodgings and service

Reconstruction of the Quadriporticus of the Theatres, in an engraving by S. L. Desprez. Facing page: House of the Golden Bracelet. Detail of a fresco with a theatrical mask.

quarters were created along the wings of the colonnade and on the upper floor. Numerous accoutrements, helmets and weapons typical of the gladiatorial contests were found here, although originally it was a space connected with the nearby theatres where the spectators could stroll during the intervals in the performances, or take shelter in the event of rain. Effectively, according to Vitruvius, in view of the length of the performances, all the theatres were expected to be equipped

The Odeion. View of the interior by T. Duclère.

E. Netti, Gladiator contest during a dinner at Pompeii.

with a spacious portico for the spectators. It also seems probable that for several years it was used as the premises of an organisation that dealt with the physical and intellectual training of youths.

(45) ODEION

This small theatre had a four-pitch roof and was probably used for musical concerts and the declamation of verse, which called for a smaller structure so as to avoid the dispersion of the sound. The Odeion could accommodate

The Odeion in a period photo.

about 1,500 spectators. It was built in the first half of the first century BC on the initiative of two *duovirs*, the same that were responsible for the construction of the Amphitheatre when Pompeii became a Roman colony.

The first seats in front of the orchestra hemicycle, which was paved with chips of polychrome marble, were reserved for the *decurions* whose seats stood on four tiers of broad tuff steps. Access to the tiered seating was via semicircular steps situated at the sides of the orchestra. On either side of the stage area, from which they could be reached, were the boxes for the guests of honour. Three doors in the stage wall opened onto the backstage dressing room and from there led directly outside.

(46) TEMPLE OF JUPITER MEILICHIOS (OR TEMPLE OF ASCLEPIUS)

An inscription in the Oscan language on the Porta di Stabia has enabled this temple to be attributed to Jupiter Meilichios. This cult reached Pompeii through the commercial links with Magna Grecia, where it was widespread. In the courtyard of the temple was an altar made of tuff from Nocera, probably dating to the third century BC.

The temple itself stood on a high podium with four Corinthian columns at the front and two at the sides, behind which was the cella. Here terracotta statues of Jupiter and Juno were found, together with a bust of Minerva, representing the deities of the Capitoline triad that were venerated in the Capitolium of the

Forum. This discovery suggests that their cult may have been temporarily transferred here after the earthquake of 62 BC, while awaiting completion of the restoration works on the main temple.

Recently an older hypothesis has been taken up again, according to which the temple may be attributed to the cult of Asclepius and Hygieia, on the basis of terracotta statues and other objects discovered within it.

Above: a reconstruction of the Temple of Jupiter. Left: the statue of Jupiter Meilichios now in the National Archaeological Museum of Naples.

The Temple of Isis, by G. Gigante.

The Temple of Isis.

N·POPIDIVS·NF·CELSINVS
AEDEM·ISIDIS·TERRAE·MOTV·CONLAPSAM
A·FVNDAMENTO·P·S·RESTITVIT·HVNC·DECVRIONES·OB·LIBERALITATEM
CVM·ESSET·ANNORVM·SEXS·ORDINI·SVO·GRATIS·ADLEGERVNT

The inscription above the entrance portal to the Temple of Isis, by K. Grob; this inscription recalls that Numerius Popidus Ampliatus financed the reconstruction of the building in the name of his son Celsinus, after the collapse caused by the earthquake of 62 AD.

(47)
TEMPLE OF ISIS

This temple, with entrance to the sacred enclosure from the street of the same name, was built between the end of the second and the first decades of the first century BC. After the damage caused by the earthquake of 62 AD it was reconstructed on the initiative of a former slave. Despite the fact that he was now wealthy he could not be elected to the council of the *decurions*, and hence he decided to finance the works in the name of his six-year-old son. This story is recalled by a plaque above the entrance door to the temple: *Numerius Popidus Celsinus, son of Numerius, rebuilt entirely at his own cost the Temple of Isis collapsed from the earthquake. For this munificence the decurions accepted him to their order without further obligation, although he was only six years old.* Isis was a goddess who consoled the suffering with the promise of salvation and happiness, and her cult, imported from Egypt, had a great following in Pompeii. The temple stands on a high podium in the centre of a colonnaded courtyard with stuccoed Corinthian columns. To the rear of the temple is a large

A reconstruction of the Temple of Isis.

93

S. Della Gatta. The Temple of Isis, Alisio collection.
Below: the Temple of Isis in a period photo.

chamber in which a marble hand was discovered together with a gold goblet, a statuette, two bronze candlesticks and two human craniums used in the religious ritual. In the left corner of the colonnade, in the part in front of the temple, is the chamber that was used for the purification rites (*purgatorium*), while the sacred water from the Nile was conserved in the basement below.

48
SAMNITE PALAESTRA

The *palaestra* or gymnasium was the headquarters of a military association of the youths of Pompeii. The building dates to the second century BC and has colonnades on three sides consisting of Doric columns made of tuff. After the earthquake of 62 AD the adjacent Temple of Isis was enlarged, reducing the area available for the gymnasium. Found here was a Roman copy of Polykleitos' original statue of Doriforus, the symbol of youth and strength.

The courtyard of the Samnite Palaestra.

49
HOUSE OF THE LYRE-PLAYER

This is an impressive building of approximately 2,700 square metres, created by joining two residences together. It took its name from the discovery of a bronze statue of Apollo the Lyre-Player. As well as this statue, magnificent paintings and portraits in bronze and marble of famous people were also found, including that of Marcellus, nephew of Augustus and patron of Pompeii. The house can be entered both from Via dell'Abbondanza and from Via Stabiana. It is arranged around two *atria* and three *peristyles*. The property, as we can deduce from the electoral propaganda and a number of graffiti discovered, appears to have belonged to the Popidius family.

The courtyard of the Samnite Palaestra.

The House of the Lyre-Player.

72
VIA DELL'ABBONDANZA

This was the main street of Pompeii and linked the Porta di Sarno with the Forum. It took its name from a public fountain with a statue of the goddess Fortuna bearing the horn of plenty. Opening onto the footpaths were numerous workshops and *thermopolia*. As a result of the damage caused by the earthquake of 62 AD, it lost its importance, and the centre of economic life of the city shifted to the crossroads between it and Via di Stabia.

Below: Via dell'Abbondanza.
Left: the fountain that gave it its name.

50
HOUSE OF THE CEII

This is a small house located on Vicolo Meridionale. The name was chosen by the archaeologists from one of the nine election slogans painted on the front wall. The rooms are decorated with paintings in the Third Style.

To the right of the *atrium*, with a fountain in the *impluvium*, is the winter *triclinium* with a painting of the young Bacchus offering wine to a tiger.

The three walls of the garden are painted with landscapes and scenes of wild beasts hunting. We can distinguish wolves chasing wild boars, a tiger chasing two rams and a lion hunting a bull, as well as a Nile landscape depicting pygmies struggling with a hippopotamus and a crocodile.

51
HOUSE OF MENANDER

This was the opulent residence of Quintus Poppaeus of the Poppaeus family, to which Nero's second wife Poppaea Sabina also belonged. It extends over 2,000 square metres and reflects the traditional layout of a Roman house, with *atrium* and *peristyle* as well as servants' and baths quarters. In the right-hand corner of the *atrium* is a *lararium*, while in the chamber on the left (opposite the *impluvium*) the walls are frescoed with a triptych inspired by the Trojan war. On the right is Laocoön, strangled by serpents along with his sons; on the left is Cassandra resisting abduction by Ulysses; in the centre is Cassandra vainly attempting to convince the Trojans not to let the wooden horse enter the city. In the right-hand corner of the *peristyle*, beyond the *tablinum*, the pavement of the living room features a mosaic panel in the centre depicting a scene with pygmies rowing a boat on the river Nile. On the walls, with a green background in the Fourth Style, are scenes of Centaurs abducting the Lapithae women. A corridor opening to the right of the *peristyle* leads to the kitchens, several basement areas and the vegetable garden. In this area a box containing 118 items of silverware, some gold objects and several coins was discovered; these had very probably been put away while awaiting completion of the restoration work on the house. From the *peristyle* we move on to the baths area, with a *calidarium* with a mosaic pavement and painted stucco on the

Cart with reconstructed wooden parts, from the House of Menander.

The House of Menander, the peristyle.

walls. At the rear of the *peristyle* are four niches, two rectangular and two apsed.

The first of these on the right, decorated with Second Style paintings, has an altar dedicated to the cult of the *Lares*, which were originally represented by five wooden or wax sculptures from which plaster casts were made. Beyond an apsed niche is a rectangular recess, on the right-hand wall of which is an image of the poet Menander seated, which gives its name to the house. Continuing along the main *peristyle* we can also observe the spacious *triclinium*. In the living room which opens on the right are the plaster casts of the bodies of twelve unlucky plunderers who had decided to visit the spot after the catastrophe of 79 AD.

The House of Menander, the atrium.

(73) ASELLINA'S TAVERN

In these premises, complete bar-restaurant facilities were discovered. On the ground floor, behind a facade covered with election propaganda, is the masonry sales counter, holding four terracotta containers for the prepared foodstuffs.

At the rear of the tavern was the staircase leading to the inn on the upper floor.

Various graffiti reveal that customers could also enjoy the company of Asellina's waitresses. We even have the names of

The exterior of Asellina's Tavern.

these assistants of somewhat easy morals – Zmyrina, Ismurna and Aegle – who even appear to have wielded a certain influence, since they were the signatories of electoral propaganda supporting candidates running for municipal offices.

LAUNDRY OF STEPHANUS

This building was a laundry and fuller's workshop (*fullonica*).
The *fullonicae* performed both the scouring of new fabrics and the washing and stain removal of used clothes. The laundry of Stephanus, named after an electoral slogan on the facade that features this name, was created

by transforming an old atrium-style dwelling. A skeleton was discovered in a basement room along with the considerable sum of 1089.5 *sesterces* in coins of gold, silver and bronze; this may have been the worldly wealth of some unfortunate passer-by who sought shelter in the laundry, or may represent the last takings of the manager himself.

To the left of the spacious entrance was a press used to fold the cloth. From here we enter the atrium with a flat roof, used to hang out the clothes.

In the peristyle behind are three intercommunicating masonry basins, and alongside five tubs where the cloth was trodden by foot. Nearby a number of vessels used to hold human urine were found, since this was utilised in the treatment of the cloth.

The urine was also collected in terracotta *amphorae* placed in secluded areas in the vicinity of the laundry. The kitchen and the latrine are located at the right-hand corner of the *peristyle*.

The atrium of the Laundry of Stephanus.

53

HOUSE OF THE LARARIUM OF ACHILLES (HOUSE OF THE SACELLO ILIACO)

Like many others, this house was being reconstructed at the time of the eruption and it is named after the Trojan chapel set at the rear of the *atrium*. In the centre of the ceiling is a medallion showing the rape of Ganymede and other scenes referring to the final stages of the Trojan War, with the episode of Hector and Achilles. The finds testify that, despite the works in progress, the house was inhabited at the time of the disaster.

54

HOUSE OF JULIUS POLYBIUS

The electoral manifestos on the facade indicate that the owner of this house was Julius Polybius, descendant of a family of freedmen. The people were exhorted to vote for him in the election to the office of *duovir*, because he would assure them "good bread". The house, dating to the second century BC is arranged differently from the typical Pompeii house, in that the entrance does not lead into the *atrium* in the normal manner, but into a rectangular chamber featuring examples of painting in the First Style.

Reconstruction of a Pompeii house. Below: the House of Julius Polybius.

55
HOUSE OF THE SHIP EUROPA

The name of the house derives from the graffito on the north wall of the *peristyle* showing a cargo ship with the name Europa, alluding to the princess Europa abducted by Jupiter in the form of a bull and carried off through the sea. The excavations carried out in 1972 by American archaeologists discovered 416 holes made by roots, identifying the former existence of an orchard and vegetable garden with a great variety of species of trees and plants. These probably included broad beans, cabbages, vines and exotic plants that arrived from the East in the imperial era: cherries, peaches, apricots and pistachios, the seeds of which were discovered in terracotta pots placed along the perimeter wall, and lemons – apparently introduced by the

Plaster casts of the victims in the Orchard of the Fugitives.

Jews and held in great regard for their medicinal properties.

56
ORCHARD OF THE FUGITIVES

This site contains one of the most dramatic and moving illustrations of the tragedy of Pompeii. An agricultural complex with a large orchard planted with vines, it has yielded the plaster casts of the bodies of 13 persons, comprising entire family groups with young people and children, surprised by the eruption of 79 AD. This field and those adjacent to it have been planted out again with the original vines, and every year wine is made from these following the vinification techniques utilised in the ancient world.

Plaster cast of a child.

Plaster casts of the victims discovered in the vicinity of Porta Nocera.

HOUSE OF THE GARDEN OF HERCULES

The original layout of the house dates to the third century BC. The bedrooms (*cubicula*) are situated at the sides of the entrance through which we enter the *atrium*. From here, a corridor leads to the large garden. Palaeobotanical investigations have shown that a variety of plants were grown in this *hortus*, all of which were of the kind used in the production of perfume, so that it has been suggested that the owner may have been a perfumier. In the centre of the eastern wall of the garden is a masonry *triclinium*, designed for dining in the open air, and next to it an altar and an *aedicula* dedicated to Hercules in which a marble statue was found.

HOUSE OF D. OCTAVIUS QUARTIUS

Despite not being particularly large, this was an extremely luxurious residence, boasting the largest garden in Pompeii, which has recently been replanted with the original trees and plants.

The house has an *atrium* with numerous bedrooms (*cubicula*) opening off it, and an *impluvium* surrounded by a low masonry flower bed. In the cubiculum on the left is a kiln used to fire terracotta vessels. In the house a bronze seal belonging to a certain D. Octavius Quartius was found, which has led to his identification as the owner of the house, previously erroneously attributed to Loreius Tiburtinus. Beyond the *atrium* is a small *peristyle*, overlooked by various other rooms.

Worthy of note here is the chamber featuring a dado in imitation marble and a double frieze: the lower part portrays episodes from the Trojan war while the upper illustrates the expedition of Hercules against Laomedon.

The back garden contains one section of the T-shaped water channel that extends along the width of the building while the second section runs the entire length of the garden. On the right-hand side of the first section of the water channel is a room with paintings in the Fourth Style. This is considered to be a chapel dedicated to Isis, in view of the image of a high-priest of Isis. On the opposite side is a *biclinium* used for dining in the open air, set at the side of an apsed fountain. On the rear wall of the *biclinium* we can admire two frescoes showing, on the left Narcissus at the fountain,

The garden of the House of Octavius Quartius.

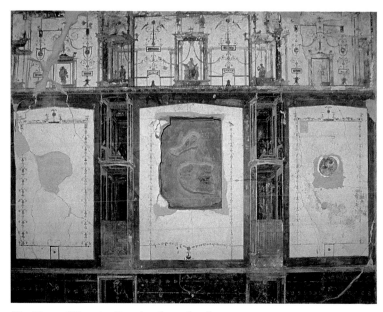

The House of Octavius Quartius, frescoed wall.

and on the right the dual suicide of the lovers Pyramus and Thisbe. The garden area, which was originally entirely covered with pergolas and enclosed all round by high trees, was used for nocturnal rites by the followers of the cult of Isis. It would appear that the two sections of water channel were used to flood the entire area in imitation of the river Nile.

(59)
THE HOUSE OF VENUS IN THE SHELL

This house, badly damaged by the Anglo-American air raids in the Second World War, has a peristyle with large-scale decorations inspired by garden elements (fountains, hedges, birds, flowers, sculpture). On the rear wall is a large painting of Venus, the protective deity of the city. The naked goddess, bedecked with golden jewels and attended by cupids, is sailing in her shell with the aid of her billowing veil used as a sail. Despite the fact that the quality of the painting is mediocre, the impression is of great scenographic effect.

The House of Venus in the Shell: the painting of the goddess in the shell.

Facing page: the House of Venus in the Shell, the peristyle.

The peristyle of the House of Venus in the Shell.

THE AMPHITHEATRE

The literal definition of amphitheatre is "the space for the spectators that runs all round the arena", but it was commonly known as the *Spectacula*, "building for performances". An inscription informs us that in 70 BC the *duovirs* Caius Quintus Valgus and Marcus Portius – the two highest authorities in the city who also built the Odeion – constructed it at their own expense. The Amphitheatre of Pompeii is the oldest and best preserved building of its kind to have survived. It could seat 20,000 people accommodated in the three tiers of seating; it was used for gladiator contests and was closed in the winter and at the

Right above: the internal corridor. Below: the amphitheatre.

height of summer. In the summer, a canopy of dark linen was stretched above the seats to protect the audience from the sun. At the top of the highest tier we can still see the stone rings into which the wooden poles used to support the awning were inserted.

This added convenience was also extensively advertised in the posters announcing the events. The upper tiers (summa *cavea*) were reached by external stairways. From a gallery running parallel to the perimeter of the arena, various staircases led to the lower and middle tiers (ima *cavea* and media *cavea*). There were two doors set on the main axis of the arena; through one of these the participants in the games entered, while the other was used to carry off the bodies of the dead and wounded. In 59 AD during a contest between gladiators from Pompeii and Nocera a violent brawl broke out between the supporters of the opposing factions, and a number of people were killed and many injured. The Senate of Rome consequently ordered the amphitheatre of Pompeii to be closed for 10 years and dissolved all the bands of fans.

After the earthquake of 62 AD the period of disqualification was reduced, allowing the gladiator contests to be revived. Nevertheless, it has to be said that the closure order was particularly severe; it seems plausible that the riot actually masked the seething resentment of Pompeii towards Nocera which had also recently become a Roman colony and had absorbed part of its territory.

This is how Tacitus recounts the episode "... [...] A futile incident caused a horrendous massacre between the colonists of Nocera and those of Pompeii. It occurred during a gladiatorial contest given by Livinèius Règulus.
As usually happens in small towns, it started out with joking that turned nasty, then stones were thrown, and in the end weapons were drawn. The people of Pompeii came off better. Numerous Nocerans were taken home

The fight between the citizens of Pompeii and Nocera, in a wall painting.

Reconstruction of the outside of the amphitheatre, from F. Niccolini.

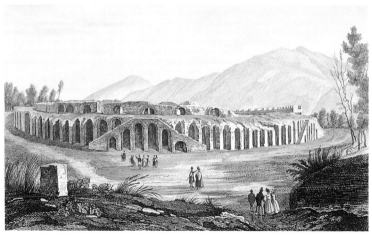

The Amphitheatre, from Zuccagni-Orlandini, 1845.

wounded or mutilated and many wept over dead sons or fathers. The Prince submitted the affair to the Senate, and the Senate referred it to the consuls.

Upon second application, however, the Senate passed a ruling banning this type of gathering in the city for ten years. Livineius and the other leaders of the sedition were punished with exile."

The Large Palaestra.

LARGE PALAESTRA

The *Palaestra* or gymnasium was the largest public space in the city and was used for sports activities. Specific imperial directives urged the young men to join *collegia iuvenum*, youth sports associations that were also used to transmit the imperial ideology, so that the function of the building was also of an political nature.

The *Palaestra* was bordered by a high wall, and access was through ten gates. It measures 141 metres by 107 and has a colonnade on three sides composed of 48 columns on the long side and 35 on the other two. In the centre is a swimming pool of 35 metres by 22.

The Large Palaestra, with the swimming pool in the foreground.

(74) PRAEDIA OF JULIA FELIX

Julia Felix, the daughter of Spurius, was the owner of this house, which on account of its large dimensions and layout can be considered as a "villa". It extends over an area corresponding to two *insulae*, two-thirds of which are occupied by a vegetable garden. After the earthquake of 62 AD, and in view of the consequent shortage of accommodation, the owner who had a talent for business decided to rent part of the property. She also found it expedient to open her private baths to the public, since in the whole city only a section of the Forum Baths was still in operation. The rental notice painted on the facade offered: *"elegant bathing facilities, shops*

The Praedia of Julia Felix: the peristyle.
Below: the garden with pool.

with living quarters above and apartments on the first floor are offered for rent to respectable people", indicating the duration of the lease as five years "from August 1st next to August 1st of the sixth year". The house was split up into various areas.

The baths, with access from Via dell'Abbondanza, were equipped with all appurtenances and an open-air swimming pool.

The apartment of Julia Felix herself looked out onto the garden, adorned with a water channel and bordered by a colonnade with precious quadrangular columns covered with marble. Then there were the shops, some on Via dell'Abbondanza and some on the side street that led to the Large Palaestra, where we can also identify the area of the house rented to tenants.

The sculptures from the garden and several of the paintings from this house are now in the National Archaeological Museum in Naples, while a fresco showing Apollo and the Muses is at the Louvre in Paris.

The Necropolis of Porta Nocera. Below: the Tomb of the Flavians. Bottom: Porta Nocera.

(62)
NECROPOLIS OF PORTA NOCERA
(63)
PORTA NOCERA

Many sepulchres are visible outside Porta Nocera. Particularly impressive is the exedra tomb of the priestess of Venus, Eumachia, to whom the namesake building in the Forum was dedicated.

Further on we come to the Tomb of the Flavians, which has eight niches above the door and another 6 at the sides, some of them bearing busts in tuff and various inscriptions. Also interesting are several tombs with high podiums, including that of Marcus Octavius

which has four niches on the facade, and that of Publius Vesonius Phileros, with a long inscription set in the centre of the podium. In the inscription Vesonius bemoans the fact that he was unjustly accused by an alleged friend. In fact we read:

"Stranger, stay a while if it is not a nuisance, and learn what it is you must guard against.
The man whose name is engraved here, whom I had hoped was my friend, accused me falsely.
In the proceedings, thanks to the gods and my own innocence, I was

The Necropolis of Porta Nocera, the Tomb of Eumachia. Below: the Porta di Nola.

The city has seven gates: one in the direction of Herculaneum and Naples, Porta Vesuvio to the north-west, one in the direction of Nola, then the Porta di Sarno to the east, Porta Nocera (or Nuceria, from the ancient name of the city) and the Porta di Stabia which at the south faced in the direction of the namesake city, and finally Porta Marina to the west, leading to the port (Jens-Arne Dickmann, Pompei, Bologna, 2007).

absolved of all charges. May he who defamed me be rejected by both the gods of the house and the gods of the other world."

64 PORTA DI NOLA

This gate faced in the direction of Nola and was built in the Samnite period by Vibius Popidus, the maximum civic authority (*meddix tuticus*) in the second century BC, as confirmed by an inscription in the Oscan language discovered on the facade of the gate.

65 NECROPOLIS OF PORTA DI NOLA

As was the practice, burial areas tended to be situated outside the city walls. Here we can see the tomb, with rectangular enclo-sure, of Obelius Firmus, an influential figure in Pompeii in the last years of life of the city. There are also two *exedra* tombs, one of them belonging to Aesquilia Polla, the wife of Herennius Calsus, a person of great influence in the city in the Augustan age.

66 HOUSE OF THE GEOMETRIC MOSAICS

This is a large dwelling with approximately 60 rooms, renovated following the damage caused by the earthquake of 62 AD. Set in a panoramic position, it has a large *atrium* with a square *impluvium*. Worthy of particular note are the remains of the *cocciopesto* paving and the beautiful mosaic with geometrical motifs from which the name given to the house derives.

67 *THERMOPOLIUM (1 8,8)*

This is a place of refreshment set on the busy Via dell'Abbondanza, Pompeii's equivalent of a "fast food" restaurant. In one of the containers recessed into the masonry counter approximately 3 kilos of coins were found, for a value of approximately 680 *sesterces*, with the prevalence of small change. The shop is completed by a small chapel dedicated to Mercury and Dionysius and a shrine for the domestic deities. The house of the restaurant owner extended to the rear of the shop and was reached through an independent entrance door opening onto the narrow side street. The *triclinium* has a superb example of decoration in the late Third Style.

The Thermopolium, I 8, 8.

GRAFFITI

One of the many graffiti found in Pompeii offers us a wonderfully expressive proof of love. It consists of the story in verse of a young girl burning with passion for her beloved, who invites the driver of the wagon that is bringing her to Pompeii to whip the horse to a gallop to reduce the time that separates her from the encounter.

"If you were on fire with love like me,
I'm sure you'd go faster!
I am in love with a handsome youth,
if only you would fly!
Go on, crack the whip,
as I've no time to lose,
now that you've had your drink,
come out and let's be off,
time is passing.
We'll go to Pompeii, and when we arrive leave me there. . . .
where this magnificent youth awaits me
if only you would fly!"

Scratched with sharp implements, traced with charcoal, sketched in red paint, the writings on the walls of Pompeii provide an extremely vivid and eloquent picture of the social, civil and political life of the city. Frequently the phrases were written by a team of pro-

Left: Rufus est. Caricature of the owner of the villa portrayed as a Caesar, from the Villa of the Mysteries.
Below: caricature profiles from the exterior of the House of the Ceii.
Bottom: male profile with superimposed phallus, from the House of the Ephebe.

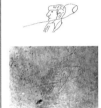

fessional scribes who enlisted the services of assistants carrying ladders and lanterns, if the operation was to be performed by night, for example during election times when the writings had to be executed in secrecy: *"Please vote for so-and-so",* or *"So-and-so is a thief".* Very often, the graffiti were merely a means of communication: *"If anyone lost a horse loaded with baskets on 26 November, get in touch with Quintus Decius Ilario, freedman of Quintus, or Lucius Decius Amfio, freedman of Lucius, beyond the bridge over the Sarno, in the property of the Mamii",* runs a graffito in another hand to notify any interested parties that the lost horse had been found and that they wished to return it to the legitimate owner. Another legend simply announces the birth of a donkey *"on the sixth of July under the consulate of Lucius Nonius Asprenas and Lucius Plotius".*
Clearly, there was no shortage of obscene messages either: *"on the ninth of September Quintus Postumius invited Aulus Attius to have a homosexual relation with me",* as well as insults, *"Queer!"* and offensive graffiti: *"Litus you're not worth tuppence, in fact you're not worth even one pence".* In short, everything and more was written up on the walls of Pompeii.
So much so that an unknown hand lamentably penned *"O walls, you have held up so much tedious graffiti that I am amazed that you have not already collapsed in ruin",* while another wrote *"May no good ever come to he who writes on this wall",* apparently oblivious to the potential repercussions upon himself.

VIA STABIANA AND VIA DI NOLA

The area comprised between Via dell'Abbondanza and Via Stabiana is the fulcrum of Pompeii, bringing together the older quarters of the city and the more recent. This district contains many luxurious residences and important public buildings, and is an area on which the commercial traffic and the urban routes converge. Via di Nola represents the northern *decuman*, and runs practically parallel to the southern *decuman* that is Via dell'Abbondanza. The *insula*e to the east of the junction with Via di Stabia are of a residential character, although there are also shops, taverns and *thermopolia*. A single public complex in the form of the Central Baths was also discovered in this district.

Reconstruction of a shop, from Niccolini.

Junction between Via Stabiana and Via dell'Abbondanza.
Facing page: the House of the Golden Bracelet, detail of one of the frescoes.

The peristyle of the House of Meleagrus.

The archaeological exhibits of Pompeii often tour the world as guests of honour at exhibitions and shows, after which they rapidly return home again. There is however an intriguing story concerning a column from Pompeii which resides permanently in Japan that is well worth telling.

The story began on 23 August 1868, when a handful of adolescents that represented the White Tiger Regiment decided to opt for collective suicide rather than submit to surrender. The Italian dictator Mussolini was so struck by this story that he decided to offer a proof of his admiration for these young heroes by donating one of the columns of Pompeii in their memory. This gift was greatly appreciated and the Pompeii column still stands proudly on the hillside of the Limoriyama park, where it is lovingly conserved. The pedestal that supports the column bears the inscription :

"In the sign of the lictors, Rome, the mother of civilisation, with this millennial column, symbol of eternal greatness, pays timeless tribute to the memory of the White Tigers. Year 1928 – VI Fascist era."

On the other side is the legend "To the spirit of Bushido, the way of the Samurai".

GLOSSARY

Apse. A recess, usually semicircular or polygonal.

Atrium. The front hall of the house.

Cavea. The semicircular tiers of seats where the spectators sat in the Roman theatres and amphitheatres.

Cocciopesto. Highly resistant flooring material made of lime mortar with crushed tile and ceramic fragments.

Compluvium. Rectangular opening in the centre of the roof of the atrium, used for lighting and to channel rainwater into the *impluvium* beneath.

Cryptoporticus. Covered gallery or subterranean passage.

Cubiculum (cubicula). Small chamber generally used as a bedroom.

Decurion. Member of a municipal or colonial senate.

Duovir. The highest magistrates, every year two were elected with both judicial and administrative functions.

Exedra (exedrae). Chamber with seats suitable for conversation. Also a small monument set upon a base with one or two steps.

Fresco. Painting executed on plaster while it is still wet.

Impluvium. Pool set in the centre of the atrium to collect rainwater.

Insula. Area of buildings between two roads, equivalent of the modern block.

Larario (lararia). Domestic shrine to the household gods.

Lavapesto. Flooring made of ground lava bound with sand and lime.

Oecus (oeci). Lounge or drawing room.

Podium. Raised platform.

Peristyle. Inner court surrounded by a colonnade.

Tablinum. Reception room situated between the atrium and the peristyle.

Thermopolium. Shop selling ready-made foods set along the street, featuring the characteristic L-shaped counter.

Triclinium. Dining room with three couches.

TO FIND OUT MORE

AA VV., *Cibi e sapori a Pompei e dintorni*, Pompei, 2005

Avvisati C., *Plinio il Vecchio*, Pompei 2001

Cantarella E. Jacobelli L., *Un giorno a Pompei*, Napoli, 1999

Dickmann J.A., *Pompei*, Bologna, 2007

Della Corte M., *Case ed abitanti di Pompei*, Napoli 1965

Fergola L., *Oplontis e le sue ville*, Pompei, 2004

García y García L., Jacobelli L. (Ed.) *Museo segreto*, Pompei 2001

Guzzo P.G. (Ed.) *Pompei, Scienza e Società*, Milano 2001

Guzzo P.G., *Storia e paesaggi della città antica*, Milano 2007

Maiuri A., *Introduzione allo studio di Pompei*, Napoli 1943

Nappo S.C., *Guida alla città sepolta*, Vercelli, 1998

Pagano M. (Ed.) *Gli scavi di Ercolano*, Pompei, 2004

Stefani G., *Menander*, Milano, 2003

Stefani G. (Ed.), *Uomo e ambiente nel territorio vesuviano*, Pompei 2003

The value of various coins from the first century AD

Aureus: 25 denari or 100 sesterces or 400 asses
Denarius: 4 sesterces or 16 asses
Sestertius: 4 asses
Ass: 1/4 of a sestertius
Quadrans: 1/16 of a sestertius

Sestertius of Caligula (37-41 AD) with laureate head and on reverse Caligula's three sisters with a cornucopia.

Aureus of Tiberius (14-37 AD) with laureate head of Tiberius and on reverse Livia seated with a sceptre.

Cover photo: *detail of wall painting from the House of the Mysteries*.
Back cover: *Via dell'Abbondanza*
Inside back cover: *excavation works in a period illustration*.
Contents page: *iengraving on shell from the Ascione Collection – Naples*.

Pompeii. Guide to the archaeological excavations
edited by Polisto Amitrano
Graphics
Nadia Bronzuto
Editorial design
Anna Maria Penna
Photos
Fotografica Foglia, P. Amitrano,

F. Cosma Colombo, G. Massimo, Archivio Fotografico Flavius.
Printed by
Cangiano Grafica
Edizioni Flavius – Pompei 2009
www.edizioniflavius.it